Competency-based Assessment

T0384795

This book is a practical, evidence-based guide for educators at all levels on how to assess and promote student learning, broadening teachers' understanding of assessment. Balancing assessment with the development and promotion of student learning can be a significant challenge for teachers.

This book provides the content, as well as practical guidance, to support educators in developing their understanding of assessment from task-driven, domain-bound content knowledge, towards the assessment of complex competencies. Supported by research, but not overwhelmed by it, the book provides practical strategies that can be applied in the classroom. The pedagogical structure of the book encourages self-guided learning, with each chapter providing opportunities for reflection to facilitate planning and goal setting, as well as quotes and vignettes from students and teachers highlighting their experiences of and perspectives on assessment.

This book is a great resource for practising educators and postgraduate students who want to improve their understanding of assessment, implement it more effectively and support better outcomes for their students.

Kate Lafferty is a Lecturer within the School of Education at La Trobe University. Kate is an experienced teacher, having worked across primary, secondary and tertiary sectors for over 24 years as both a generalist teacher and Gifted Education specialist and taught at the postgraduate level at Monash University. She has delivered numerous professional development sessions and presented at international conferences.

Melissa Barnes is an Associate Professor and the Associate Dean of Learning and Teaching in the School of Education at La Trobe University. Her teaching focus and research interests are situated within the fields of teacher education, pedagogy, assessment, policy and English language learning. Melissa is trained as both a primary school and an English as an Additional Language (EAL) teacher and has taught in schools in the US, Germany, Vietnam, Brunei and Australia.

Competency-based Assessment

Evidence-based Insights and Strategies for Educators

Kate Lafferty and Melissa Barnes

Routledge
Taylor & Francis Group

LONDON AND NEW YORK

Designed cover image: Metamorphosis of a Butterfly © Myron Jay Dorf/Getty Images

First published 2025
by Routledge
4 Park Square, Milton Park, Abingdon, Oxon OX14 4RN

and by Routledge
605 Third Avenue, New York, NY 10158

Routledge is an imprint of the Taylor & Francis Group, an informa business

British Library Cataloguing-in-Publication Data
A catalogue record for this book is available from the British Library

ISBN: 978-1-032-65720-2 (hbk)
ISBN: 978-1-032-65719-6 (pbk)
ISBN: 978-1-032-65721-9 (ebk)

DOI: 10.4324/9781032657219

Typeset in Galliard
by codeMantra

Content

Figures and tables

Figures

Tables

Preface

Our competency-based assessment journey began in 2019 when Kate, who was teaching in an independent school, reached out to Melissa, whom she had taught alongside in several initial teacher education subjects at a large Australian university. Like many other educational journeys, it began with a problem that needed to be addressed. Kate and her school colleagues were part of a team tasked with re-imagining their school's Year 9 program and they were trying to figure out how to *meaningfully assess Year 9 student learning in a way that recognised the combination of knowledge, skills, behaviours and values that often remained invisible in school assessment tasks.* Sparked by student research into OECD's Sustainable Development Goals[1] and using the design thinking methodology,[2] there was a sense that students were often not explicitly being assessed on the transferable knowledge and skills that reflect everyday living and work. The problem was that there was no way of assessing these competencies in any meaningful way.

The first project commenced in 2019, with secondary students leading the co-construction of competency-based assessment frameworks that were then discussed and validated by other key stakeholders, such as teachers and those who represent real-life working contexts (e.g., industry representatives). Since then, a team of teachers within the school have worked in a collaborative practice group (CPG) to continue to unpack and explore ways in which the frameworks can be introduced and used with and by students for learning. The second project (a longitudinal study) commenced in 2023 and focuses on designing, trialling and refining a range of competency-based assessment frameworks in secondary school settings, while also exploring how these frameworks support teacher planning and instruction and student learning as they track their learning progress. We provide an overview of the research methodology as much of this work has prompted the writing of this book.

Designing a co-constructed framework[3]

This first project aimed to collaboratively develop or co-construct an assessment framework that incorporated key workplace competencies. The identification and description of these competencies was led by a group of secondary students and validated through stakeholder engagement with teachers and industry representatives. The student-designed frameworks, inspired by the OECD's enterprise skills, outlined eight competencies (creativity, critical thinking, digital literacy, communication, teamwork, problem-solving, presentation skills and financial literacy). Initially, Year 9 students began to develop the framework, working in groups and conducting research on the different competencies. The industry representatives and teachers were later involved to ensure the frameworks' relevance to real-world workplace skills and academic skills, respectively.

The qualitative project captured a variety of participant experiences and perspectives on competency-based assessment in education and utilised the following methods:[4]

1 Task response. Students, teachers and industry representatives were given an opportunity to break down the competencies into knowledge, skills, behaviours and values.
2 Focus groups—Reference groups. Once the students had used class time to research, design and discuss the development of the frameworks, these were examined by a teacher reference group and an industry representative focus group. In these reference groups, they worked together to merge their individual inputs into the students' frameworks, balancing educational objectives and workplace relevance. The aim of the session was to come to a consensus on the descriptors and evidence provided in the framework. This methodological approach used collaborative engagement across student, teacher and industry groups to facilitate an exchange of ideas and ensure the frameworks' robustness and transferability.
3 Focus groups—Collaborative groups. The participant groups were equally distributed (students, teachers and industry representatives). They were once again asked to examine the frameworks, discuss and come to a consensus on what should be provided in the frameworks.

This project provided the foundation for created frameworks that were then further examined and tested.

Longitudinal study: Pilot study

Given that the teachers at the school had continued to discuss and explore ways to use the rubrics (2021–2022), we initiated a longitudinal study in 2023[5] that would examine:

1 The utility of the frameworks (e.g., How user-friendly are they? How consistently interpreted and applied are they?).

2 The psychometric properties of the frameworks (e.g., To what extent do they discriminate amongst different student groups, represent the intended construct and provide a logical, progressive order?).

In collaboration with the teachers in the CPG, we focused on five of the original eight frameworks:

- Communication
- Creative thinking
- Critical thinking
- Problem-solving
- Teamwork

The first year of the project encompassed collecting detailed assessment task descriptions from the ten participating teachers that explained the conditions under which tasks were carried out, as well as student achievement data relating to the relevant frameworks. Teacher and student questionnaires and teacher and student focus groups were conducted to examine the utility, value and accessibility of the frameworks. Additionally, industry focus groups were conducted to discuss the frameworks' relevance to industry needs and their views on the use of competency-based assessment in education.

This book will draw upon the empirical research from these studies to frame the arguments made.

Use of generative AI

In the writing of this book, we recognise both the potential and the ethical concerns that have been raised in using generative AI for research and writing.[6] For this purpose, we want to disclose how we have used generative AI, namely ChatGPT, as a tool to prompt language structures that represent our knowledge and thinking. We provide an example of how we used ChatGPT to identify prompts that students might use to gain feedback on their writing (see Chapter 6). We have also used ChatGPT to help in combining key ideas to start structuring scenarios (e.g., a student who is in Year 5, who is neurodiverse) and these have been crafted by us to provide an example of what we are trying to demonstrate. We have also used ChatGPT to help us in identifying plain and concise language for key definitions and for rephrasing unclear sentences.

Why read this book?

Competency-based assessment is increasingly being implemented in school systems around the world to reflect the knowledge and skills needed for the future.[7] Despite this, assessment practices that support the teaching and tracking of the knowledge, skills, values and behaviours which are needed for the future are often sidelined by more immediate concerns about improving standardised test scores and implementing current agenda reforms. However, an understanding of competency-based assessment, we argue, is valuable for teacher candidates, educators, researchers and policymakers as they consider the what, why, when and how of their current assessment practices and how future-proof these practices are. The introduction of generative AI is one example of how beliefs and practices about assessment will ultimately need to adjust to reflect the real-life contexts in which we live, study and work.

We also argue that purpose, practice and progress are key ideas that underpin effective assessment and are reflected in this book. Knowing the purpose of assessment is essential in any context, but understanding the purposes of assessing competencies relies on intentional practice. Applying small changes to existing practices facilitates a greater awareness of how we can determine current levels of development for our students, but also how we can provide opportunities for them to progress. This book unpacks each of these aspects in a practical and accessible way.

Notes

1 https://sdgs.un.org/goals.
2 https://dschool.stanford.edu/resources/getting-started-with-design-thinking.
3 Barnes, M., Lafferty, K., & Li, B. (2024). Assessing twenty-first century competencies: Can students lead and facilitate the co-construction process? *Educational Review*, *76*(4), 691–709.
4 Monash University Human Research Ethics Committee (Project ID:26752).
5 La Trobe University Human Ethics Committee (Project ID: HEC23117).
6 UNESCO, IRCAI. (2024). *Challenging systematic prejudices: An investigation into gender bias in large language models.* UNESCO. https://unesdoc.unesco.org/ark:/48223/pf0000388971.
7 Tan, J.P.L., Koh, E., Chan, M., Costes-Onishi, P., & Hung, D. (2017). *Advancing 21st century competencies in Singapore.* National Institute of Education, Nanyang Technological University, Singapore.

Acknowledgements

We would like to acknowledge the role of our research-practice partnership and the commitment and passion that teachers have shown towards learning about and embedding competency-based assessment in their school setting. We thank the students who contributed their voices and leadership at various stages of the project. We look forward to continuing this work.

We are very grateful to our critical friends, Victoria Giummarra, Heather Westwood and Pete Westwood for their feedback on each chapter. As experienced and impactful teachers, your insights and suggestions have been incredibly valuable in shaping the published version. We also extend our appreciation to Annie Lafferty, our assistant, in the final stages of preparing the manuscript.

1   What is assessment?

When you hear the word *assessment*, what comes to mind? It tends to stir up a range of different emotions because each of us had unique experiences of assessment. While assessments are used for a range of purposes and contexts, we believe that assessment is an essential and powerful part of the learning and teaching process. However, we acknowledge that, for some, assessment is viewed as a punitive and inequitable gatekeeper as it becomes the judge of whether you have the knowledge and skills deemed important at that time.[1] While assessments are often used as gatekeepers to determine, for example, who enters a particular school and/or university program or who successfully completes secondary/high school, this book focuses on how assessment can be integrated into the learning and teaching cycle to improve student learning and inform teaching practices.

Assessment is understood and practiced in a wide range of ways, across schooling contexts and amongst teachers. When trying to make sense of the connections between assessment and learning, assessment is often characterised in four distinct ways, exemplified by their distinctive purposes. This section attempts to define these four assessment purposes and exemplify them through teaching scenarios.

- **Assessment of learning (AoL)** is summative in nature, with the purpose of assessment being to judge and measure student performance and outcomes using formal tasks.

In the following scenario, Mr. Anderson's use of AoL aligns with his intention to assess the knowledge his students have obtained at the end of a unit.

Box 1.1

Mr Anderson wants to assess whether students have acquired and/or mastered the knowledge and skills deemed important for understanding chemical reactions at the end of the unit. The assessment task involves a

---

DOI: 10.4324/9781032657219-1

comprehensive written test, where students must explain various chemical processes, balance equations and apply their knowledge to solve real-world problems. The test is designed to cover the key concepts emphasised during the unit.

- **Assessment for learning (AfL)** is formative in nature, and is about improving and shaping (*forming*) teaching and learning processes and practices to support student outcomes. *Both* students and teachers are involved in the process and actively seek, interpret and apply evidence to improve student learning.
- **Assessment as learning (AaL)** is also formative in nature, but AaL requires increased student ownership as the purpose is to actively engage students in self and peer assessment.

The following scenario captures how Ms. Chau uses both AfL and AaL as assessment strategies to guide learning and teaching processes.

Box 1.2

Ms. Chau is committed to using Assessment for Learning (AfL) and (AaL) strategies to enhance learning and teaching processes in her Year 6 classroom. The focus is on a unit about ecosystems. Ms. Chau begins the unit with explicit instruction, covering key concepts, scientific vocabulary and the interconnectedness of living organisms within ecosystems. Students create concept maps to visually represent their understanding of ecosystem components and share these with their peers. This serves as a formative tool for both self-assessment and peer evaluation. Based on this formative evidence, Ms. Chau conducts mini lessons to address specific misconceptions or expand on topics of interest. She reflects on common misconceptions and areas where additional support may be needed. Students also maintain reflective journals where they record their reflections on each lesson, questions they have and strategies they use to overcome challenges. Ms. Chau holds individual conferences with students to discuss their reflective journals, set learning goals and provide personalised guidance.

- **Diagnostic assessment** is neither summative of nor formative in nature but rather proactive. The purpose of this assessment is to determine what students already know about a topic, skill, concept or behaviour in order to inform the use of teaching strategies and support learning processes.

In the final assessment scenario, Mrs. Thompson utilises diagnostic assessment strategies to support student learning and plan for teaching.

Box 1.3

Mrs. Thompson recognises the importance of diagnostic assessment to understand her students' prior knowledge and tailor instruction effectively. The focus is on a new unit about multiplication. Before formally starting the multiplication unit, Mrs. Thompson administers a diagnostic test. This test includes a mix of basic multiplication problems, word problems and questions about related concepts like addition and subtraction. Mrs. Thompson incorporates hands-on activities and group discussions related to multiplication to observe how students approach mathematical problems and communicate their understanding. She also conducts brief one-on-one interviews with select students to gain insights into their thought processes and identify any gaps in foundational knowledge.

Understanding assessment purposes and the roles of teachers and learners

Assessment of learning, or AoL, is heavily practiced in schools as it has been traditionally used to determine, judge and compare student achievement. Assessment data are primarily analysed by teachers (and school leaders) to determine where individual students and cohorts of students are situated in light of the school's curriculum and/or school/state/federal benchmarks. Evidence[2][3] suggests that formal assessment tasks have been used by teachers and school leaders to:

- document and compare student performance and achievement in and across schools,
- select students for subsequent levels of education and
- keep principals and teachers accountable.

It is important to recognise that most students (and parents) place a high value on assessment, which influences how they understand and value particular learning tasks.[4] This impacts students' decision-making about what learning is important and how they see themselves being involved in the assessment process. AoL is often associated with assessing the key knowledge and/or skills that are deemed important by teachers, students and parents. Unfortunately, the knowledge and skills that are assessed in more formal AoL assessments are often viewed as having more value than the knowledge and skills assessed in formative assessment tasks (collaborative learning, critical thinking, etc.). This is problematic as most summative tasks cannot feasibly assess all knowledge and skills and, therefore, only reflect a narrow subset of the knowledge and skills taught and learned. Key knowledge and skills have been prioritised by what is deemed important at that particular time and what is practical to assess. For example, multiple-choice tests are much easier to mark but they are also very difficult to validly design and/or provide opportunities for the application of key knowledge. Therefore, what is assessed in summative assessments, which tend to be more valued by teachers, learners and parents, do not necessarily reflect what learners should know and learn over time. Such assessments intend to measure achievement at an 'end point' (a period, unit, or term) but this does not provide a clear understanding of how learners progress and learn key knowledge and skills over time.

As a result, there are concerns that many of the assessments used within schools, particularly standardised testing instruments, are not always fit for purpose[5] and do not always factor in the role of student learning in the assessment process. Assessment for Learning (AfL) and Assessment as Learning (AaL) position students as more active participants in the assessment process. AfL requires *both* students and teachers to be involved in the process as they both actively seek, interpret and apply evidence to improve student learning. AaL, on the other hand, positions students as relevant assessors as they participate in metacognitive and self-regulated learning strategies to assess both their work and others'.[6] Not defined as 'endpoint' assessments, as is AoL, AfL and AaL assessments are often administered during the learning process.

Like the other types of assessment, diagnostic assessment is often defined by when it is administered—the start of a topic, lesson or unit. These assessments are used to collect assessment data on what students already know about a topic, skill or behaviour and are used as a benchmark to track students' progression in learning. The data are used for teacher planning rather than for reporting student achievement.

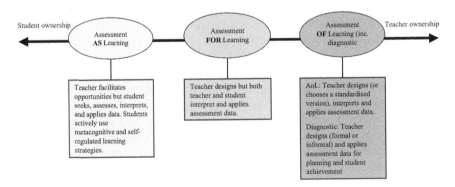

Figure 1.1 Continuum of typical ownership.

These four different purposes of assessment can be located on a continuum of ownership in which teachers and students *typically* possess different levels of ownership in the assessment task. We acknowledge that assessment is discussed in a range of ways, such as formal to informal, traditional to alternative, and nested to stand-alone (see Chapter 3 for more about these assessment perspectives), however, Figure 1.1 attempts to demonstrate how assessment purposes often position teachers and students in relation to assessment (see Chapter 6 for more about the role of learners in the assessment process).

The 'search for evidence of learning' is not bound by stages of teaching and learning and involves both teachers and students

While AoL, AfL and AaL have traditionally been used to understand the different purposes of assessment, we argue that these terms, at times, distract from the overarching purpose of assessment, which is the search for evidence of learning.[7] The search for evidence of learning involves collecting and interpreting information that helps determine the level of knowledge and skills that students possess. Student learning progresses over time so we must assess frequently, providing learners with multiple opportunities to demonstrate their learning. This is, therefore, not defined by when the assessment occurs and who is involved but acknowledges that educators must seek evidence of learning formally and informally, summatively, diagnostically and formatively. As educators, we must continue to gather and interpret assessment **data** and **evidence** to inform the learning and teaching process. We argue that to ensure that assessment is positioned in a way that will inform teaching practices and improve student learning, there are three key aspects to consider when searching for the evidence of learning:

1 Assessment, regardless of who designs, collects or interprets it, is the process of searching for *evidence* of learning. This requires collecting and interpreting assessment data rather than making inferences about student learning.
2 The search for evidence of learning is not limited to a particular stage within the teaching and learning cycle. While AoL often focuses on the endpoint of learning, and AfL and AaL align more with diagnostic and formative assessments, we argue that the search for evidence of learning is not confined to a stage but can happen throughout the teaching and learning cycle.
3 Teachers cannot validly collect, interpret and apply evidence of student learning without actively engaging students as they are central actors in the process of learning and, therefore, the process of assessment.

'Evidence' is a term that is often used in education, particularly in the use of 'evidence-based teaching'. Evidence-based teaching refers to the use of empirical research and scientific evidence to inform and improve learning and teaching practices. The use of evidence in the context of assessment suggests that there is proof of student learning, both achievement and progression, rather than inferences about student learning.

To ensure that the evidence of learning that is collected truly reflects student progress and achievement, we must consider the **validity** and **reliability** of the assessment. Assessment validity and reliability are often discussed in light of the design and evaluation of assessments. For an assessment to be valid, it must measure what it is designed to measure. In doing this, any interpretations and actions made from the assessment are intended to be both meaningful and appropriate. Validity can be understood in relation to 'truth.' Does an individual's performance in the assessment provide a truthful representation of their knowledge, skills and/or behaviours? When thinking of validity, we must also consider construct validity. In the case of assessing reading, we might ask ourselves, "Does the assessment reflect the theoretical foundations or **construct** (e.g., the building blocks of how we understand a learner reads) that it is supposed to measure?" For example, we both remember, early in our teaching careers, when we were elementary/primary teachers, we were encouraged to use **running records** to assess our students' reading ability. However, we noticed that the construct validity of this assessment was compromised when assessing students from language backgrounds other than English. This was because, at times, the errors were due to pronunciation rather than reading ability. In this case, while the purpose of the test was to measure the construct of reading, it was also measuring other variables, such as pronunciation, which called into question whether the test was measuring what it intended to measure. As discussed, while validity relates to 'truth' or what is being measured, reliability relates to 'consistency.' Consistency in this context refers to student performance across tasks and time as well as scoring (across markers/raters and by individual raters).[8] The importance of quality evidence (including reliability and validity) is further discussed in Chapters 2 and 5.

A developmental approach to assessment

As a result of educational experiences and current views of assessment, teachers, students and parents often think of the *products* of learning (scores on a test, an oral presentation, a written assignment or project, etc.) when thinking of assessments. These products attempt to demonstrate one's knowledge and skills and primarily focus on an 'end point' of one's learning rather than the *process* or the incremental *progress* of learning. Typically, traditional assessments have focused primarily on measuring achievement or the mastery of knowledge and skills at a particular point in time rather than seeing learning as a continuum of knowledge and skills. A developmental approach to assessment, on the other hand, attempts to move away from focusing on student achievement as an 'end point' to viewing assessment as incremental and positive development over time. This is not to be confused with developmental assessment, which is the process of mapping and comparing a child's performance with other children of the same age.[9] In addition, we push back against deficit views of learning which focus on what students are lacking. Instead, we focus on what students can do and are ready to learn next. We view assessment as a way of supporting students in identifying and understanding the pathway (or learning progression) to progress in their learning. To do this, teachers must track and monitor student development over time. However, in order for teachers to scaffold students in their development, there needs to be a clear understanding of what the different levels of progression or growth involve and how a student can progress from beginner to advanced on this continuum.[10]

The continuous and frequent search for evidence of learning is an essential factor when adopting a developmental approach to assessment. Teachers must be able to interpret assessment data to locate students on the learning progression and identify tangible learning objectives to ensure that students continue to develop or progress. The focus shifts from measuring a nominated 'end-point' to assessing progress over time. These developmental stages in one's learning provide critical and tangible steps for *both* teachers and students. For teachers, these steps allow them to identify where their students are in their learning and where and when they need to provide additional explicit instruction (and/or re-teach certain concepts, skills or behaviours). They can determine where students are, where they are going and where they have been. This is important in being able to communicate progress to both students and parents/carers.

A developmental approach is seemingly at odds with how *knowledge* has been traditionally taught and understood. Key knowledge and information are explicitly taught and then obtained or mastered (through a process of explicit instruction and retrieval practices). Skills, attitudes, values and behaviours, on the other hand, have often been treated differently and often sit outside of the notion of 'knowledge'. It is assumed that they will be taught implicitly. It is the silo-ing of these different domains—knowledge, skills, attitudes values and behaviours—that limit their transferability to applying them in future studies and employment. In contrast, competencies do not silo these domains but focus on the interconnectedness of the key knowledge, skills, attitudes, values and behaviours that are needed for educational and workplace contexts. We argue that competencies can and should be explicitly taught and assessed. Not only can they be incrementally developed from an early age but they are increasingly important for the future.

What are competencies?

We define **competencies** as the knowledge, skills, attitudes, values and behaviours students need to thrive in and shape their world, whether that be in future studies, employment an/or active participation as a global citizen. They have also been referred to in the following ways:

- soft skills[11]
- practical intelligence[12]
- enterprise skills[13]

- twenty-first-century skills[14]
- general capabilities[15]

Competencies are complex and multidimensional due to the *interconnectedness* between knowledge, skills, attitudes, values and behaviours. It is this complexity that allows individuals to enhance their capacity to respond to ever-changing environments and take action to shape their own, as well as collective, futures. In our research over the past several years, we have examined, unpacked and empirically tested a number of competencies, creating frameworks with incremental learning progressions that have been used to assess students' development in:

- Communication
- Critical thinking
- Creative thinking
- Problem-solving
- Teamwork
- Professionalism
- Self-regulated learning

Box 1.4

To unpack these ideas, let's look at how 'communication' might be understood as a competency. Use the following prompts to consider how communication might be defined, observed and developed.

- What comes to your mind when you think about what makes someone good at communication (written, oral, multimodal, etc.)? What do they know? What do they do?
- Think of an example of when you demonstrated strong communication skills. What was the context? What did you think, say or do? What aspect of communication did you excel at and why? Is there any example of when you could have communicated better? Why? What would you have done differently?
- Consider how you have developed your ability to communicate with others. What aspects have you tried to develop and how?

While most of us have likely developed communication skills in more implicit ways (e.g., learning from our own mistakes or through observations of others), we can all agree that communication is important in all facets of life. While we acknowledge that communication skills, in one form or another, are discussed and/or developed in educational institutions, we argue that they are not always *explicitly* taught and assessed.

While a focus on competencies has begun to make its way into educational reform documents in countries like Australia[16] and Germany,[17] there is still limited understanding of how these competencies can be explicitly taught and assessed.[18] This is one of the key motivators in writing this book.

Why should the teaching and assessment of competencies be prioritised in the school curriculum?

We acknowledge that teachers are often navigating educational reforms, including curriculum changes, leading to increased workload.[19] So, when we argue for explicitly teaching and assessing competencies in schools, some educators might think, "Oh, please no, not something else." The idea of another thing to teach and assess is not only overwhelming but unpalatable. However, before we explain how this can be done in schools in ways that enhance what is already being done (rather than an add-on), we need to consider *why* competencies should be taught and assessed.

They will equip our young people to navigate the future

Education reforms often aim to solve or address existing 'problems' in education.[20] While this is important, sometimes this distracts from proactively considering and anticipating ways to future-proof our education system. In our longitudinal pilot study with industry representatives, several participants explained why competencies were so important for schools. Their perspectives remind us that today's industries and companies must utilise competencies, such as critical thinking, problem-solving and creative thinking to have a competitive edge. However, they argue that as industries rely on competencies to prepare for and navigate the future, schools, too, must be preparing young people:

> So, one thing that I've been trying to advocate for is critical thinking and problem solving for kids…so a bit of context: I work for the CSIRO [Commonwealth Scientific and Industrial Research Organisation] but in the technology innovation space. So, in terms of the skills of the future, when you think around stuff that AI can do versus what humans do, this is still a very key skill, problem solving and critical thinking, and even more so in the future. So yes, I'm certainly an advocate for it.
> (Industry representative, focus group 1, 2023)

> What I've experienced working both in Australia and internationally is that, and increasingly as emerging technologies are going to be adopted, human creativity and creative thinking is going to be the key differentiator between us and the robots. I think what is really important though is if I think about the next generation of people in the workforce, leaders, executives, their ability to join the dots which contextualise what is it that is a problem….
> (Industry representative, focus group 2, 2023)

Industry representatives view the development of competencies in schools as key to equipping young people with the types of thinking that only humans are able to do. Despite many educational institutions focusing on how to prevent students from using Gen AI to write their essays, the participants, who represent industry, are arguing that education needs to focus on developing the skills that Gen AI cannot replicate rather than focusing on the skills that Gen AI can.

They will help in supporting a needed shift from the product of learning to the process of learning

There has always been an intense focus on the product of learning, with achievement scores being the key to success. While most educators acknowledge that the processes of learning are important, limited time is spent helping students think about and consider how they will incrementally progress in their learning. While one Year 7 student, in our longitudinal study, describes how teachers can only focus on the product of learning rather than the process because of how many students they have, another student expresses her desire to develop more than just content knowledge.

> … there are too many students to focus on how they [students] worked [process], its more about what they did [product].
>   (Year 7 student, focus group, 2023)

> We should be trying to develop these skills and not just to develop our knowledge of the content which is what they assess already but to improve the process with how we do in the subject.
>   (Year 7 student, focus group, 2023)

While the students acknowledge that assessing (and explicitly teaching) the process of learning is time-consuming for teachers, students see the value in learning, applying and progressing in the thinking processes and learning strategies needed to do well in their studies.

They provide important foundations for individual well-being and the well-being of society[21]

The Organization for Economic Cooperation and Development (OECD) established the 'Future of Education and Skills 2030 project in 2015 to help guide countries in shaping future-proof education systems. The result of this work identified competencies related to innovation, problem-solving and autonomy that will help students succeed throughout their lives.

How can they be implemented in schools?

In our longitudinal pilot study, which aims to explore how competencies are taught and assessed in a secondary school setting in Australia, we have and continue to pilot the use of developmental rubrics (more on this in Chapter 5), which we have named 'competency frameworks' to identify, test and refine appropriate student-friendly language that helps both teachers and students track the development of key competencies over time. The project aims to examine the utility of the framework regarding user-friendliness, while also exploring the teacher and student perspectives and experiences of using them.

One of the key findings in our first year of the pilot study revealed that teachers found that for students to effectively develop these competencies, the frameworks needed to be explicitly introduced:

> I think it helps for them [students] to be explicitly aware of it [the framework] at the time that they're learning. Because certainly, in my case, they found it very difficult to make those connections after the fact. And I think they probably hadn't noticed or appreciated that learning that had happened during, whereas they might have, had I actually introduced the framework beforehand.
>
> (Teacher, focus group, 2023)

When the competencies were explicitly taught, the participating students argued that:

> it [the competency...in this case 'teamwork'] was more noticeable, and you paid more attention to it....
>
> (Year 10 student, focus group, 2023)

While some have argued that competencies cannot be explicitly taught,[22] we disagree and the findings from our study would support this conclusion. Firstly, competencies cannot be arbitrarily or loosely linked to what students are learning without making the connections between subject matter and the competency clear and explicit. If the aim is to help students develop and progress in these competencies, they need to be able to understand:

1 what the competency is (e.g., understanding its characteristics),
2 how learning this competency links to their learning (e.g., relevance) and
3 what the pathway is to develop the competency (e.g., identifying where they are on the framework and being able to identify what to work towards).

The explicit instruction of key competencies allows for better retention over time as the competency needs to be broken down into manageable pieces and allow students to have a greater understanding of each indicator or trait while understanding the connection between them. In addition, as discussed earlier in the chapter, there are varying levels of teacher and student involvement in the assessment process. We argue that competency-based assessment requires student involvement in the learning process. Developing key competencies will support learners not only in their learning during their schooling but also in their future studies and future employment. Therefore, students need to take ownership of these competencies earlier rather than later so they can self-regulate their learning in future situations.

Another key finding that was revealed in the first year of our pilot study is that there is a widely held misconception that certain competencies can only be linked to certain discipline areas (e.g., problem-solving in maths and creative thinking in arts). However, if we only teach certain competencies with certain subjects, we are missing rich opportunities to make these competencies transferable and meaningful. The students in our study argued that competencies were more like learning strategies and that they could be used for a range of different subject areas:

> Maybe some might use problem-solving in English and others use creative thinking in Maths like people use different strategies to get them to learn.
>
> (Year 7 student, focus group, 2023)

Despite some students viewing competencies as helpful learning strategies, a few students felt that certain competencies were more meaningful or better linked to certain discipline areas (see Chapter 6 for more on this).

Practical and empirical perspectives

This section aims to further explore some of the key concepts and ideas that have been discussed in this chapter but from two different perspectives—the empirical and the practical. Firstly, teachers' assessment beliefs and practices will be explored by examining a recent study of how assessment is currently understood and enacted in school settings in Australia. Secondly, this section will also provide an opportunity to examine what is meant by validity and reliability through the use of assessment scenarios.

A look into teachers' assessment beliefs and practices

Several studies have examined the ways in which teacher beliefs influence their assessment practices.[23][24][25] Teachers' knowledge, skills, beliefs and dispositions about assessment are referred to as their *assessment literacy*. Brown and colleagues interviewed 22 Australian teachers to explore their assessment literacy and how this influenced their assessment practices. They wanted to know (1) what teachers knew about assessment as a concept, (2) how they applied assessment practices in their various socio-political contexts and (3) how they interpreted data to engage students in learning. Their study found that teachers' beliefs, and subsequently their practices, were heavily influenced by state and institutional assessment policies. In government schools in Australia, most teachers' beliefs about assessment were shaped by recommended assessment practices from the state government (e.g., the use of on-demand **Common Assessments Tasks** [CATs]).

It is important to note that teachers' beliefs about assessment can be shaped by a range of different factors, including their own experiences with assessment (the good and bad), assessment policies shaping their school context (federal, state or institutional) and/or professional development opportunities. However, there are, at times, tensions between their understanding of how assessment practices should be applied and what practices are expected in their local school context. Brown and colleagues examined how teachers described the differences in assessment practices between the junior years (e.g., Years 7–10) and the senior years (Years 11–12). The participating teachers in this study recognised that the senior years focused primarily on testing, with a focus on testing discrete knowledge, while the junior years focused more on skill-based learning. Despite one teacher arguing that assessment should be more skill-based, she recognised the trickle-down effect from the senior school, which focused on 'testing,' to the junior years. These practices were becoming increasingly expected and encouraged through the use of CATs. Therefore, there was a conflict between the teacher's personal conception of assessment and the assessment practices encouraged by the state government and school. Their study suggests that while teacher beliefs (and their conceptions of assessment) influence assessment practices, assessment practices are often bound by or shaped by federal, state and institutional recommendations.

Regarding teachers' roles in interpreting and communicating assessment data, the participating teachers in their study felt that they were accountable more to parents and students than to schools or governments. They had to be ready to communicate why a student received the mark they did, which had an influence on how they interpreted assessment data. However, one teacher admitted that she and her colleagues did not understand the learning continuum which made it difficult to scaffold students to progress.

This study highlights that there are clear tensions between teachers' assessment beliefs, their practices and the expectations of their socio-political contexts. We argue that although assessment is an important aspect of teachers' work, there is a need to further examine and understand how assessment beliefs and practices impact student learning.

Practical applications: Applying understanding validity and reliability to assessment scenarios

To help in understanding and then applying what is meant by validity and reliability in assessment, use the following activity to identify any concerns you might have regarding the validity ('truth') or reliability ('consistency') of the following assessment tasks:

1 Students listen to a 15-minute video lecture and take notes. The teacher makes individual comments on each student's notes.
2 Students are given a sheet with ten vocabulary items and directed to write ten sentences using each word. The teacher marks each item as

acceptable/unacceptable and students receive the test sheet back with items marked and a total score ranging from 0 to 10.

3 Health and Physical Education students are given an end-of-unit multiple-choice exam on basketball skills which is 100% of their mark for the term. Students are given a score only.

4 Due to the history teacher becoming annoyed about not understanding some students' writing, he has asked students to take a grammar quiz to assess students' grammatical knowledge (not part of the history unit). Scores are given online and are 20% of students' final mark.

5 Students give a five-minute prepared presentation on a particular topic. The teacher evaluates by filling in a rating sheet, indicating the student's success in delivery, content and language.

The following are some notes that may help you as you consider the validity and reliability concerns in many classroom assessments. It is important to note that it is difficult to ensure that an assessment is entirely valid and reliable but we should always consider the validity and reliability of the assessments that we design or choose to use in our classrooms. This is a theme that will be revisited throughout the book.

Scenario 1:

- Validity: Students may vary in their note-taking abilities so there would need to be clear understanding (and explicit teaching) of what good note-taking looks like and what is expected.
- Reliability: The teacher's comments may be inconsistent across different students' notes and if more than one teacher is marking, they may take on different approaches (how much feedback and what they focus on) when providing feedback.

Scenario 2:

- Validity: Writing ten sentences might not be enough to thoroughly assess understanding.
- Reliability: The criteria for acceptability lack clarity, leading to inconsistent marking.

Scenario 3:

- Validity: A single exam may not be representative of overall skills and knowledge in basketball. This is a good example of when the 'construct' of basketball and the skills required may not be validity assessed through an exam (as it would need to be assessed by physically demonstrating the skill).
- Reliability: A single exam could be affected by factors such as test anxiety, a student having a bad day and poorly worded multiple-choice questions.

Scenario 4:

- Validity: While history may require students to express their understanding through written responses, having a quiz on grammar that contributes to 20% of the students' overall marks may result in their overall scores not being a truthful representation of their historical knowledge and/or understanding.
- Reliability: A single quiz (as opposed to several over time) could be affected by factors such as test anxiety, a student having a bad day and poorly worded multiple-choice questions.

Scenario 5:

- Validity: Five minutes may limit the depth of the presentation and limit their ability to demonstrate what they know about the topic.
- Reliability: Providing consistency in rating across different presentations may be a challenge, particularly if there are a large number of presentations.

Chapter summary and reflection

Though assessments often act as gatekeepers in educational and professional contexts and conjure a range of emotions, this book focuses on integrating assessment into the learning and teaching cycle to enhance student learning and inform teaching practices. We first examined how assessment is often categorised into four distinct purposes: Assessment of Learning (AoL), Assessment for Learning (AfL), Assessment as Learning (AaL) and Diagnostic Assessment. However, we must understand and examine assessment in ways that extend beyond these four purposes. Not only should assessment be viewed as the search for the evidence of learning, which is not bound by *when* it occurs in the learning and teaching cycle, but it should also attempt to avoid the continual silo-ing of knowledge, skills, attitudes values and behaviours. A focus on competency-based assessment allows for meaningful links between assessment, learning and teaching, with a focus on supporting learners to understand and make decisions about how they can track and progress in their learning. In addition, a competency-based assessment approach acknowledges the interconnectedness between knowledge, skills, attitudes, values and behaviours and views knowledge as foundational and key to the transferability and applicability of competencies.

To help consolidate and internalise what you have read in Chapter 1, reflect on the following questions:

1 What are your current beliefs and practices regarding assessment?

- What assessment concepts come to your mind when you think about your own teaching practices (formative, summative, etc.)?

- How are your assessment practices shaped by your own experience, your teaching context (your local teaching context, state or federal requirements, etc.)?
- How do you go about interpreting and communicating student progress?

2 What are your experiences in using a developmental approach to assessment? What are your experiences using competency-based assessments? What are the opportunities and challenges that you can identify when using competency-based assessments in your teaching context?

3 When considering ownership of the assessment process (see Figure 1.1), where would you put most of your assessments on this continuum? If you wanted to change your current approach, what might you do?

Notes

1 Barnes, M., & Cross, R. (2022). Standardized testing as a gatekeeping mechanism for teacher quality. In I. Mentor (Ed.), *The Palgrave handbook of teacher education research* (pp. 1–18). Springer International Publishing.

2 Cumming, J.J., Van Der Kleij, F.M., & Adie, L. (2019). Contesting educational assessment policies in Australia. *Journal of Education Policy, 34*(6), 836–857. https://doi.org/10.1080/02680939.2019.1608375

3 Klenowski, V. (2011). Assessment reform and educational change in Australia. In R. Berry & B. Adamson (Eds.) *Assessment reform in education* (pp. 63–74). Springer.

4 Brown, T.D., Barnes, M., & Finefter-Rosenbluh, I. (2024). Teacher perspectives and experiences of assessment literacy in victorian junior secondary schools. *Australian Journal of Education, 68*(1), 5–22. https://doi.org/10.1177/00049441231214022

5 Baird, J.-A., Andrich, D., Hopfenbeck, T.N., & Stobart, G. (2017). Assessment and learning: Fields apart? *Assessment in Education: Principles, Policy & Practice, 24*(3), 317–350. https://doi.org/10.1080/0969594X.2017.1319337

6 Schellekens, L.H., Bok, H.G., de Jong, L.H., van der Schaaf, M.F., Kremer, W.D., & van der Vleuten, C.P. (2021). A scoping review on the notions of Assessment as Learning (AaL), Assessment for Learning (AfL), and Assessment of Learning (AoL). *Studies in Educational Evaluation, 71*, 101094.

7 Griffin, P. (2017). *Assessment for teaching.* Cambridge University Press.

8 Darr, C. (2005). A hitchhiker's guide to reliability. *Set: Research Information for Teachers, 3*, 59–60. https://doi.org/10.18296/set.0623.

9 Bellman, M., Byrne, O., & Sege, R. (2013). Developmental assessment of children. *British Medical Journal, 346*, 31–35.

10 Griffin, P. (2017). *Assessment for teaching.* Cambridge University Press.

11 Chiu, K., Mahat, N., Rashid, B., Razak, N.A., & Omar, H. (2016). Assessing students' knowledge and soft skills competency in the industrial training programme. *Review of European Studies, 8*(1), 123–133. https://doi.org/10.5539/res.v8n1p123

12 Joseph, D., Ang, S., Chang, R., & Slaughter, S. (2010). Practical intelligence in IT: Assessing soft skills of IT professionals. *Communications of the ACM, 53*(2), 149–154. https://doi.org/10.1145/1646353.1646391

13 Chang, J., & Rieple, A. (2013). Assessing students' entrepreneurial skills development in live projects. *Journal of Small Business and Enterprise Development, 20*(1), 225–241. https://doi.org/10.1108/14626001311298501

14 Deng, L., & Zhengmei, P. (2021). Moral priority or skill priority: A comparative analysis of key competencies frameworks in China and the United States. *Comparative Education*, 57(1), 83–98. https://doi.org/10.1080/03050068.2020.1845063

15 Australian Curriculum, Assessment and Reporting Authority [ACARA]. (2024). General Capabilities (Version 8.4). https://www.australiancurriculum.edu.au/f-10-curriculum/general-capabilities/

16 Ibid.

17 Kultusministerkonferenz [Standing Conference of the Ministers of Education and Cultural Affairs of the Federal Republic of Germany]. (2000). *Rahmenvorgaben für die Einführung von Leistungspunktsystemen und die Modularisierung von Studiengängen [Framework for the introduction of credit point systems and the modularization of degree courses.].* Retrieved 5 January 2024, from http://www.kmk.org/fileadmin/Dateien/pdf/PresseUndAktuelles/2000/module.pdf

18 Barnes, M., Lafferty, K., & Li, B. (2024). Assessing twenty-first century competencies: Can students lead and facilitate the co-construction process? *Educational Review*, 76(4), 691–709.

19 Heffernan, A., Bright, D., Kim, M., Longmuir, F., & Magyar, B. (2022). 'I cannot sustain the workload and the emotional toll': Reasons behind Australian teachers' intentions to leave the profession. *Australian Journal of Education*, 66(2), 196–209.

20 Barnes, M., & Cross, R. (2021). 'Quality'at a cost: The politics of teacher education policy in Australia. *Critical Studies in Education*, 62(4), 455–470.

21 Organization for Economic Cooperation and Development. (2019). OECD Future of Education and Skills 2030. Project Background. https://www.oecd.org/en/about/projects/future-of-education-and-skills-2030.html

22 Sweller, J. (2022). *Some critical thoughts about critical and creative thinking.* https://www.cis.org.au/wp-content/uploads/2022/03/ap32.pdf

23 Brown, T.D., Barnes, M., & Finefter-Rosenbluh, I. (2024). Teacher perspectives and experiences of assessment literacy in victorian junior secondary schools. *Australian Journal of Education*, 68(1), 5–22. https://doi.org/10.1177/00049441231214022

24 Looney, A., Cumming, J., van Der Kleij, F., & Harris, K. (2018). Reconceptualising the role of teachers as assessors: Teacher assessment identity. *Assessment in Education: Principles, Policy & Practice*, 25(5), 442–467. https://doi.org/10.1080/0969594X.2016.1268090

25 Xu, Y., & Brown, G.T. (2016). Teacher assessment literacy in practice: A reconceptualization. *Teaching and teacher education*, 58, 149–162.

2 Learning and assessment design

Teachers spend a lot of time planning what they will teach. Schools may allocate planning days throughout the year or have time at the end or start of the year to plan what will be taught. When teaching in primary schools, our experiences usually meant drawing upon an established scope and sequence chart to ensure we covered the curriculum and then assigning someone or a pair to develop the planning for the term. Those responsible for the area, planned different levels of activities and resources and provided these for the team. In a secondary setting, our experiences were similar, but the division of planning was based on topics or units within subject areas.

As we reflect on our planning practices, whilst at times it seemed somewhat prescriptive, there was also flexibility in how we taught the content. Differentiation was planned for based on generalised 'above', 'at' and 'below' levels. The differentiation for our individual students and their unique learning needs occurred in our own weekly planning. However, the timing of the content delivery within a unit of work was often 'fixed' due to the pressures of covering the planned curriculum, as well as ensuring assessment timelines were adhered to. Through both experience and observation, these combined forces often led to an unrelenting tension between the 'plan' and the learning needs of students.

Capital 'A' assessment

Assessment in most of our planning experiences was discussed in terms of being an endpoint, where the teaching and learning reach their destination and signpost the move to the next topic. From our research, there appear to be at least two ways that teachers, and students, talk about assessment that reflect this: assessment with a capital 'A', and assessment with a lowercase 'a'. Capital A assessment reflects the 'endpoint', the oftentimes single task or activity that students complete to demonstrate what they have learnt during the unit. The identifying features for this type of assessment usually came in the form of student questions, such as "Will this be on the report?" or teacher conversations

DOI: 10.4324/9781032657219-2

about the task in terms of when the 'Assessment' will be scheduled or the number of 'Assessments' for the term.

Of course, this type of Assessment is summative and can be influenced by additional pressures of reporting timelines, accountability and the school's perspective of what constitutes 'evidence' of learning.

Alternatively, there is lower-case 'assessment': the assessment that occurs when we check and course-correct student learning. There appears to be less discussion around this type of assessment, whether it be between teachers and students or amongst colleagues.

The difference between *Assessment* and *assessment* seems to reflect a mindset that permeates classrooms and learning. It creates a tunnel vision of working towards the Assessment, that is, the summative assessment task that goes on the report. If a task is not summative, reported on and shared via the school's reporting process, its value to the students is often diminished. Assessment essentially defines the curriculum as students focus on what they think they need to learn to be successful on a test.[1] But this sets up a situation that limits students' ability to demonstrate what they know and can do as the summative task becomes the one piece of evidence used to ascertain their level of performance.

> If it's a task that's not assessed (to go on the report), I don't work as hard on it; I don't try as much.
>
> (Year 11 student, conversation, 2024)

When it comes to **competency-based assessment**, particularly for complex competencies, the one-off summative task does not seem to work. Our research with teachers in assessing these competencies highlighted that it is just not feasible to attempt to assess all aspects of the competency in one task at one moment in time. Instead, there needs to be a much more deliberate approach that provides multiple opportunities for students to demonstrate, and for teachers to observe, the competencies in action.

When we consider the assessment piece of our planning, we need to consider the situations that will provide students with an opportunity to demonstrate their understanding. This means having the right 'tool' for the job. Imagine you are hiring a painter to paint your house externally. This could be considered a high-stakes decision as the cost of painting can be high. Before you make a decision, you contact three different painters and ask each painter to show you how well they can paint. You provide the paint and the brushes for the 'trial'. One painter comes on a really hot day, with full sun on the area they are painting. The second painter comes on a day that is mild and overcast, and the third painter you provide with a toothbrush because the other two painters accidentally took the brushes home. The first painter ends up with cracked and peeling paint, so you eliminate them as an option. The third painter took too long to paint the same area as the others and the finish was not great. The results from the second painter were perfect so you hire them for the job.

While this example is a bit ridiculous, it illustrates how the design of assessing a painter's competence was inherently flawed by the selected tools and context. Painter 3 was disadvantaged as the tool used to assess their skills was inappropriate. Painter 1 was disadvantaged because the context of the assessment (i.e., the weather conditions) compromised their results. The same thing can and does happen in a learning situation (usually without a toothbrush!) where the design of the assessment does not align with the type of learning that is being assessed.

This is where learning design and assessment design come into play. Learning design is

> the description of the teaching-learning process that takes place in the unit of learning. The key principle in learning design is that it represents the learning activities and the support activities that are performed by different persons (learners, teachers) in the context of a unit of learning.[2]
>
> (p. 13)

By this definition of learning design, assessment design is embedded as it can be considered an activity that supports learning. This reflects the importance of consistency between the learning and assessment activities.

Alignment

Alignment occurs when there is consistency amongst all the elements of learning design,[3] that is, what teachers want students to learn (learning objectives); the ways in which they will teach it (learning design); the ways in which the student will learn it (learning experience) and the ways in which student learning and development will be evidenced (learning assessment). Figure 2.1 illustrates the relationship between each of these elements. The associated guiding questions for each element highlight a key shift in the assessment mindset, with a focus on process rather than product. For there to be alignment in learning and assessment design, there needs to be a focus on the *skills*, the learning for which the teacher is measuring, rather than a focus on the *task* itself. This means that any assessment criteria should reflect valued competencies (skills, knowledge, attitudes), and not just task-specific content that may not be repeated.

Consider the following example. A Year 3/4 teaching team are developing a unit on narrative writing. The assessment task will be a narrative that is written in a timed session. The students are provided with a picture of a deserted beach as a stimulus. The assessment criteria incorporate the following:

1 Includes beach in story
2 Includes 3/2/1 characters

3 Is 400/300/200 words long
4 Has x number of grammatical/spelling errors

These criteria are focused on the product of the task itself. In no way do they represent the skill of crafting a narrative or understanding of the structure of a narrative. If we return to our painters, it would be like basing their performance on how many houses they have painted. They may have painted a lot, but the quality is terrible because they rush the job.

Learning and assessment design will mean different things to teachers and students. For teachers, learning design defines what is to be learnt and sets out the plan for teaching and learning activities that will scaffold and develop student learning. On the other hand, for students, it is the assessment design that defines what is to be learnt, and this may or may not be explicit. The broad goal will always be the same – that there is a developmental change; or, in other words learning will occur.

Learning design

The days of planning a sequence of learning based on a selection of teachers' favourite activities have been replaced with a much more intentional backwards design approach to learning design. While the templates used and the level of detail in the early stages of the design may vary, teachers will typically begin by determining the endpoint – what is it that we want students to learn and be able to do at the end of the sequence? Ways of determining the degree to which students meet those objectives are identified through the assessment tasks and lastly the teaching and learning activities are planned. The questions from Figure 2.1 provide a useful scaffold for working through the learning design:

1 What do we want students to learn/develop?
2 How will we know if they have learnt it? What does this look like?
3 What is the best way for them to learn this?

We can draw on a well-known backward design model, Understanding by Design (UbD), to identify further questions that we need to consider when planning our learning design.[4] The sequence of the steps forces us to address learning **and** assessment design at the outset, as shown in Figure 2.2.

What do we want students to learn/develop?

For many schools, mandated curriculum documents influence, if not determine, the objectives for a sequence of learning. Domain-based knowledge, skills and understandings are identified and perhaps taxonomies such as Bloom's[6] or Structure of Observed Learning Outcomes, (SOLO)[7] are drawn

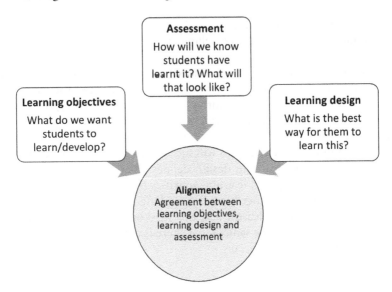

Figure 2.1 Alignment.

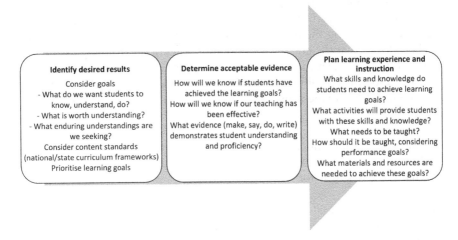

Figure 2.2 Understanding by Design (adapted from p. 18).[5]

upon to create objectives that move beyond declarative knowledge (i.e., facts or information) to procedural knowledge (i.e., processes, skills, procedures). Declarative objectives involve knowing 'what', such as knowing that the capital of France is Paris or the definition of photosynthesis. On the other hand, procedural objectives involve knowing 'how' to perform tasks or carry out processes like solving a maths problem or conducting a science experiment. Learning designs should reflect a balanced approach that incorporates both types of knowledge. Declarative knowledge helps students grasp foundational concepts, while procedural knowledge equips them with the skills to apply and use that knowledge effectively in various contexts. Competency-based learning and assessment design requires both, knowing what to do and knowing how to apply it.

Determining the 'what' of complex competencies, whether it be a general capability or other competency, tends to be an afterthought. Connections to the 'main' content are looked for once the 'real' learning has been identified. In our experience, the focus on the competency tends to be more of a 'tick the box' exercise to indicate that the content descriptions of the competency have been covered. Of course, this is not always the case. There are a number of collaborative partnerships globally that are prioritising competencies, such as New Pedagogies for Deep Learning,[8] Center for Curriculum Redesign,[9] New Metrics[10] and the OECD's transformative competencies.[11] There are also many schools (and students) that are recognising the value and role of competencies for learners and have developed their own bespoke suite of competencies.

> We should be trying to develop these skills and not just to develop our knowledge of the content which is what they assess already but to improve the process with how we do in that subject. But then that would be a way for us to just develop those skills, really.
>
> (Year 7 student, focus group 2023)

To develop competencies effectively, there needs to be intentionality in teaching and learning. We liken it to the development of any other type of skill, like riding a bike or learning to read. There can be an assumption that we develop our capacities in these areas, such as communication or teamwork, through osmosis; that it will just happen along the way through our experiences and interactions. Whilst this is true to a point, development will largely stagnate or be left to happenstance depending on environmental and intrapersonal factors. We can use running as an example. Children typically learn to crawl, walk and then run. For most, that is where it might stay. But a child may commence a program like Little Athletics. As they compete against themselves (personal bests) and their peers, and progress through the age groups, they are coached to improve their running technique – the way they move their arms, their cadence, and how to use blocks to start a race. Without targeting these aspects of running, their development as a runner will be hindered. Potentially, they may develop from watching others but to ensure development, it needs to be intentionally and explicitly taught.

For competencies, like critical and creative thinking, we need to be explicit and specific about the 'what,' as was demonstrated in the running example.

This can be difficult to identify as it requires an understanding of the competency itself. If we want to include collaboration as a learning objective, we need to know what aspects of collaboration we are focusing, on whether it be reaching a consensus, engaging with other perspectives, or taking on group roles. There also needs to be an awareness that learners will be at different stages of their development within each competency. Just as they have different learning needs in maths or writing and reading, we need to be aware that rolling out a one-size-fits-all approach will not do the job effectively. Our learning design needs to allow for variation in what our learners can do and are ready to learn next.

This is not necessarily an easy task, particularly when first beginning to work with a focus on competencies. Where there are curriculum documents to support teachers' understanding of the learning progression through each learning domain, the understanding of how competencies are constructed and developed is less understood. Recent research with primary school teachers from New South Wales indicated that many teachers do not understand the **general capabilities** of the Australian Curriculum, and that 71% of the teachers surveyed either did not use or only occasionally used general capability strategies.[12] Where general capabilities (critical and creative thinking, ethical understanding, etc.) were addressed, it was largely through incidental and informal opportunities.

A way of addressing this gap is to draw on a framework that provides guidance on the developmental progression and what to plan for. Curriculum scope and sequence charts from the relevant jurisdiction offer a useful starting point. Chapter 5 will provide detailed guidance on how to use this as a basis to develop a tool for planning, teaching, learning and assessing.

Figure 2.3 provides a template for planning based on the **Understanding by Design**[13] backwards design model. In identifying the learning objectives, we have provided prompts to consider not just the knowledge content but also competency-focused objectives through transferable core competencies. By categorising objectives in this way, the difference between the two is highlighted and the need for balance is emphasised.[14] When planning core competency learning objectives, consider the skills independently from any context. For example, if the focus is on Communication, then the transferable competencies may be *conveying meaning/arranging ideas and concepts for clarity* and *adapting delivery for the context*. The explicitness of these statements provides teachers and learners with an awareness of specific skills that will be developed. As the statements are not linked to a context, it promotes the transferability of these skills. This is not always readily understood or accepted. See Box 2.1 for a discussion on transferability.

Learning intentions: (what do I want students to learn?)	
Core competencies (transferable)	*Knowledge for action (application)*
E.g., Deliver messages effectively and efficiently, using language that is accurate, concise, and easy to understand. Tailor communication style and content to the specific needs and interests of the audience.	

What fundamental ideas or theories do I hope students remember well beyond the details?

What competencies (constructs) will be developed through the big idea?

□ Creative thinking   □ Problem solving

□ Critical thinking   □ Communication

□ Teamwork

Evidence: (how will I know students have learnt it?)
- What will students do, say, make or write to demonstrate competence?

Empowering Learners, Building Bridges:
How can students actively shape their learning journeys and assessments? Can we connect them with external resources to fuel real-world relevance and growth?

Performance assessment planning – evidence of learning

Consider the following when designing or using an assessment activity:
1. **Define your goal:** What are you trying to achieve with this performance task, and what evidence do you need to prove it?
2. **Gather evidence:** How will you collect data to assess student learning? What tools or assessments will you use, and at what point?
3. **Track progress:** How will you capture and document the evidence you collect?
4. **Make sense of the data:** What does the evidence tell you about student understanding and achievement?
5. **Take action:** How will you use the insights gained from the evidence to inform future teaching and learning?

Performance tasks	Supporting evidence of learning per task
• Assesses **competencies** covered in the learning area, not just specific tasks • Provides detailed feedback on competency development, not just task completion **using criterion-referenced rubrics** • Connects directly to the learning goals defined above • Ensures the task allows for diverse abilities and performance levels • Gives students a chance to put their learning into practice • Provides different ways for all students to participate and succeed	• Who provides feedback on the task? Is it just the teacher, or are students and peers also involved? (Highlights involvement and feedback diversity) • Does this assessment go beyond this specific task? Could it be used later on for portfolios or tracking progress over time?

Figure 2.3 Planning template based on UbD incorporating complex competencies

Box 2.1   Can we take our skills with us?: Exploring the transferability of competencies

There is an underlying assumption throughout this book that complex competencies are transferable. Transferability, in the context of learning and applying competencies, refers to the ability to effectively use knowledge, skills and attitudes acquired in one situation in new and different situations. It essentially serves as the bridge between what we learn and how we utilise it across various contexts, subjects and challenges.

Think of it like this: when you learn to ride a bike, you gain not just the specific skill of balancing and pedalling but also broader principles like coordination, spatial awareness and problem-solving. These broader skills are transferable to other activities, like skateboarding or surfing. The more transferable your learning is, the more adaptable and versatile you become as a learner.

You may be reflecting on how these competencies apply to your teaching and associated disciplines. In our research, we have experienced conflicting views from both teachers and students on the applicability of competencies in various domains. For some, there were restrictions on what competencies applied to certain subjects based on the nature of the subject and task. Consider the two student quotes below.

> I think creative thinking would probably apply like with history or English but with maths I feel like it's working with concepts that we know, it's not fluid enough to be creative with 'cause you still have an answer to get to. For example in a maths test.
>
> (Year 10 student, focus group, 2023)

> I feel like for maths creative thinking is actually crucial 'cause you have the process of being creative, you'll reach the answer even though that answer is absolute but you still use a creative process to reach it.
>
> (Year 7 student, focus group, 2023)

The first student had particular ideas about the nature of learning in Maths based on her perspectives of how understanding and knowledge were constructed. And whilst they both acknowledged that the objective was to provide 'the answer', the second student focused more on process, rather than product (i.e., the answer). These quotes typify the contrasting views and the implicit beliefs influencing those views.

Transfer of learning occurs all the time both in and out of school contexts.[15] The concepts learnt in a maths class are transferred and applied in a physics class. The skills developed in formulating questions in an English class are used in a science class. The same can be applied to competencies. Our ability to think critically in History will draw on the same fundamental skills when thinking critically during a science experiment. Focusing on the process, rather than the product, emphasises the characteristics of the same competency in different contexts.

But transfer does not just happen without some effort on the part of the learner and the teacher. As the quotes illustrated, implicit beliefs about the nature of the discipline and the competency will influence the degree to which transfer can happen. It is easier for students to transfer their learning when they see similarities between the contexts in which the competency is being used and developed. This is known as **near transfer**,[16] the applicability of the skills is easily observed (e.g., the maths and physics example). **Far transfer** is where the competencies are used in significantly different contexts and situations.[17] This requires deliberate effort and adaptability.

Transfer does not just vary in the 'distance' between the two contexts, it also varies in how it happens. **Low road** and **high road** transfer are two distinct ways in which previously learned knowledge or skills can be applied to new situations.[18] These pathways differ in terms of the level of effort and deliberate processing involved. **Low road transfer**, also known as 'reflexive' or 'automatic' transfer, happens when previously learned skills are automatically triggered in response to familiar stimuli or situations. It is a fast, unconscious process that does not require much cognitive effort. This type of transfer is most common for well-practised skills, routines and habits that are embedded in our procedural memory. Think of it like riding a bike or driving a car. Once you've learned how to do it, it becomes automatic. Unsurprisingly, low road transfer is observed in near-transfer situations, where the new context is very similar to the original learning environment.

On the other hand, **high road transfer** ('mindful' or 'flexible' transfer) requires the conscious and deliberate application of previously learned knowledge or skills to new and unfamiliar situations. It requires effort in active reasoning, problem-solving and adaptation. High-road transfer is more demanding, but it allows for greater flexibility and creativity in applying knowledge to diverse situations. It is typically observed in far-transfer situations, where the new context is significantly different from the original learning environment. An example of this is being asked to use your understanding of gravity, learned in science class, to explain how a satellite stays in orbit. This requires connecting and adapting existing knowledge to a new context.

What is the best way for them to learn this?

Let's return to our Year 3/4 teaching team planning their unit on narrative writing. They have determined their learning objectives and are beginning to discuss the learning experiences they will employ. The term 'learning experience' describes all of the activities, planned or spontaneous, that are used with the intention of developing students' skills and understanding. To promote the development of competencies, we can integrate six characteristics within and across our planned learning experiences.[19]

1 Higher-order thinking processes are used to extend and deepen understanding of content and issues,
2 Issues or areas of study are viewed from multiple perspectives using a cross-disciplinary approach,
3 Academic capabilities are integrated with personal capabilities,
4 Meaningful and student-centred that provide challenge and scope for action,
5 Have a transformative, impactful element, contributing to local or global issues,
6 Flexible settings drawing on digital tools and enhanced connectivity.

Drawing on research will ensure we are providing the conditions that we need for transfer to occur so that our students can apply their developing competencies in different areas of learning.[20] When designing learning experiences consider how they

Develop depth of understanding amongst learners.

- Provide opportunities to
  - grasp concepts and skills thoroughly in the initial learning context.
  - engage in meaningful learning experiences that promote deep processing.

Focus on principles and patterns.

  - Identify underlying principles and patterns that can be applied broadly.
  - Seek connections and commonalities across different domains.

Promote practice and reflection.

- Provide opportunities to
  - engage in deliberate practice and apply the competency in a range of contexts.
  - reflect on experiences to solidify understandings and identify transfer opportunities.

Identify similarities and differences across contexts.

- Provide opportunities to
  - bridge the gap between familiar and new situations by pointing out connections.
  - adapt knowledge and skills while recognising distinct elements of new contexts.

Explicitly teach for transfer.

- Build in opportunities to

  - highlight transfer opportunities and strategies during instruction.
  - provide examples of transfer in action across different domains.

Encourage metacognition.

- Provide opportunities to

  - reflect on own learning processes and transfer strategies.
  - reflect on how knowledge is both acquired and applied.

Create varied learning contexts.

- Provide opportunities that

  - expose learners to diverse challenges and scenarios that encourage transfer.
  - require students to apply skills in meaningful, real-world settings.

The teaching and learning activities used to develop and practice competencies need to be meaningfully embedded in the planning. In aligned teaching, where all components are consistent and support each other, students are engaged in appropriate learning activities. Cowan describes this as "the purposeful creation of situations from which motivated learners should not be able to escape without learning or developing" (p. 100).[21] A lack of alignment somewhere in the system allows students to escape with inadequate learning. This requires an understanding of the competency and how it typically develops which then allows for knowing what to look for in the search for evidence of learning, i.e., assessment.

The final question to address when aligning our learning design is the assessment piece. What evidence do we need to be able to make judgements about student learning and whether the learning objectives have been met? Assessment design is not just about coming up with a task or suite of tasks that we will use to collect this evidence. It is also about ensuring that the assessment design will provide us with quality evidence.

Assessment design: How will we know if they have learnt it? What does this look like?

Assessment design refers to the intentional and systematic process of planning, creating and organising tools and methods to measure a person's knowledge, skills, abilities or other relevant attributes. This process involves determining the *purpose* of the assessment, defining the specific learning outcomes or goals to be assessed, selecting appropriate assessment instruments or tasks, establishing suitable criteria and deciding on the methods for inclusive and fair data collection and analysis. Effective assessment design considers the context, target audience and desired information, ensuring that the assessment *aligns* with the learning objectives.

Evidence-centred assessment design is based on the idea that assessments are designed by focusing on the skills, knowledge and understandings and the associated behaviour or performance that demonstrate these attributes.[22] This approach poses several questions including:

1 What are we measuring?
2 How do we measure it?
3 Where do we measure it?
4 How much do we need to measure?
5 How is evidence accumulated across tasks?

There is also the question of how we determine the quality of the evidence. While we often hear of terms like validity and reliability for this (see Chapter 1), we can unpack this a bit more by considering whether the evidence is:[23]

Valid:

• Has the learning outcome been considered?
• Is the task consistent with the purpose of the assessment?
• Is it at an appropriate level?

Sufficient:

• Is there sufficient evidence to enable an accurate level of competency? (i.e., avoids the shopping list approach)
• Is there a balance of direct and indirect evidence?

Authentic:

• Is this the student's own work?

Current:

• The work is of the current student at the current time.

Consistent:

• The evidence has been collected over time and in different contexts to ensure there is consistent demonstration of competencies in the learning outcomes.

Box 2.2 provides a summary of key aspects of assessment design to consider when aligning learning experiences and assessment practices. One of the first questions to consider is why the assessment is being conducted. In working with teachers in both consultative roles, and as part of teaching teams, it was surprisingly common that the question of purpose was not addressed. For example, weekly spelling tests were rolled out without question with a Grade 2 class, including the ways in which the words were assigned to students. When asked about the purpose, no one really understood the reasons behind it. The issue of fairness and bias is also crucial to address to ensure there are no barriers for students to demonstrate what they know and can do (see Chapter 4). All of these factors need to be considered from the beginning.

Box 2.2   Key aspects of assessment design

When designing and planning for assessments as part of the learning design, consider the following aspects.

Purpose

- *Clarity:* Defining learning objectives clearly is crucial. What specific knowledge, skills, or behaviour changes do you aim to assess?
- *Alignment:* Assessment tasks should directly align with the learning objectives they measure. Misalignment can lead to inaccurate evaluations.

Methods

- *Variety:* Use diverse assessment methods like exams, projects, presentations, portfolios, discussions or observations to provide multiple means of expression and action and assess multiple aspects of learning.
- *Relevance:* Choose tasks that mirror real-world situations or apply learning in meaningful contexts.

Feedback

- *Formative:* Incorporate assessment as a continuous learning process where feedback helps students refine their understanding and improve performance.
- *Summative:* While formative feedback guides growth, summative assessments like final exams or grades provide snapshots of overall learning achievement.

Ethical considerations

- *Fairness:* Assessments should be accessible and inclusive for all learners, considering diverse backgrounds and abilities.
- *Bias:* Minimise potential for bias by using clear criteria, objective rubrics and multiple forms of assessment.

Using the characteristics in Box 2.2, reflect on the types of assessment tasks that you have used with students or that you have completed yourself. What did these tasks demand of students? Were they focused on recall information (e.g., multiple-choice questions, true/false)? Did they require the application of knowledge and understanding (e.g., essays)? We can draw on the same models and taxonomies that were used to develop learning objectives to help us unpack and inform our assessment design (i.e., Bloom's Taxonomy, SOLO) and Miller's Model of Clinical Competence.[24]

These models are useful in that they provide a framework of cognitive complexity (e.g., Bloom's, SOLO) as well as the level of competence (e.g., Miller's Model of Clinical Competence). Bloom's and SOLO are familiar for most teachers. The verbs in both models describe cognitive complexity leading to more complex learning objectives and provide both teachers and students with observable behaviours that reflect developing competence and frontload procedural, or functioning, knowledge. We can then use these verbs to help design assessments that elicit these deeper levels of understanding and competence so that learning is assessed in terms of quality and depth. There are many resources freely available online that identify the range of verbs applicable to the levels of each model. SOLO provides a similar approach in that it identifies different levels of understanding, ranging from not yet understanding through to surface knowledge, deep knowledge and conceptual or constructed knowledge. As with Bloom's, SOLO taxonomy identifies verbs to indicate the level of complexity and understanding of the learning.

Where Bloom's and SOLO are useful in considering the cognitive complexity of learning and assessment design, Miller's approach is helpful when it comes to assessing practical performance. It was designed as a model of clinical competence and is relevant to developmental competency-based assessment. Someone may 'know' what it means to think critically, they may also be able to tell you how to go about applying critical thinking skills, but this doesn't mean they can do it. Miller's work identifies four levels that a student will work through in their developing competence.[25]

1 Knows: This is the basic level of knowledge acquisition, where learners can recall facts and concepts.
2 Knows how: Learners can apply their knowledge to solve problems and make decisions in simulated settings.
3 Shows how: Learners can demonstrate their skills and knowledge in real-world situations under supervision.
4 Does: Learners can independently perform their duties in actual practice settings without supervision.

Often, our assessment design addresses 'knows' and 'knows how' but stops there. Vocational Education and Training (VET) courses are examples of where learning and assessment design utilise each of these levels of learning. In VET programs, learning is defined by 'units of competency', with each unit beginning with a verb. For example, the Victorian Certificate of Education (VCE) VET program in Health includes units such as:

–   Communicate and work in health or communicate services (CHCCOM005)
–   Organise personal work priorities and development (BSBWOR301)
–   Follow basic food safety procedures (HLTFSE001)

The unit names themselves highlight the difference between knowing and doing. Where a student may be able to recite the guidelines and regulations for food handling and safety on a test, this does not automatically assume they will be able to apply it in context. When planning to assess competencies in schools, we need to ensure that our design allows students to apply their skills by showing and doing. Ultimately the best way of doing this is through performance tasks (see Chapter 3) which by their very nature will elicit the behaviours of the targeted competency (if designed appropriately).

This comes back to the mindset shift with a focus on process rather than product. The focus on process will typically lead to a focus on competence. A shift from the capital 'A' assessment event to planning and identifying multiple opportunities for students to demonstrate what they can do will lead to more reliable and valid recognition and more targeted teaching. But this raises another question of consistency.

How much is enough?

Capital 'A' assessments, those assessments that we refer to as the assessments for the term (or semester), are often one-off summative events. They are typically awarded a grade in a secondary school setting. In primary settings, it is less typical to see a list of assessment tasks on a report; instead, the assessments are used to locate learners on the learning continuum with a grade assigned using the relevant authority's grading scheme. In some cases, such as Victoria, the grading scheme is at the school's discretion but must include a five-point scale[26] whereas New South Wales[27] and Queensland[28] offer a common letter grade scale that differentiates between levels of knowledge and competence. The terms 'typically', 'very high', 'thorough' and 'sound' appear in the prescribed levels and this raises the question of 'how much is enough'? How much evidence is required for teachers to decide where learners are currently located on the developmental continuum?

Take a moment to reflect on the degree of evidence you need to be confident in making a judgement. Consider what 'typically' means to you. We often hold implicit ideas about what terms like *typically* or *sound* mean, without discussing this with colleagues, students or parents. Some teachers, students and parents alike may equate *consistently* or *typically* with *always*. That students must demonstrate 100% accuracy in whatever they are being assessed on. But this doesn't quite make sense. One hundred per cent accuracy 100% of the time is not realistic. We all have 'off' days; times when we are unwell, distracted, unmotivated or confused by the nature of the task. We know that reliability requires consistency across time, tasks and markers and that there will always be variation in the tasks themselves. A reasonable target to work towards for 'typically' is what they do most of the time, with room for mistakes. One-off assessment tasks do not allow for judgements to be made about consistency across time and tasks. This reinforces the need to build multiple opportunities for learners to demonstrate what they know and can do to allow for the collection of quality evidence that is reliable and valid.

This does not mean that there is a need to collect masses of evidence of student learning. This can lead to issues of usefulness and interpretation, as well as the risk of over-assessing and placing less focus on teaching. The answer is ultimately a professional judgement and will vary from context to context. What is required is a clear understanding of what is being assessed and why, and ensuring there is sufficient coverage of the skills, knowledge and understandings you are assessing to establish a consistent pattern of student competence. This includes having a range of easier items and more difficult items, or elements of the task, to provide students with an opportunity to demonstrate their competence without any **ceiling** or **floor effects** getting in the way of this.

Case study: Outdoor Education: Teamwork

This chapter has addressed many aspects of learning and assessment design with a focus on competency, alignment and opportunity. This section details a case study from our research with teachers working with competency-based assessment for the first time.

The following lesson overview was developed for a Year 10 Outdoor Education program focusing on one competency, teamwork. The school identified this competency as being an important area to develop and recognise and is trialling ways of embedding explicit teaching and assessment of these skills. The teacher planned for *multiple, explicit opportunities* to teach the associated skills and understandings of teamwork. The nature of the task, planning and participating in two outdoor trips, meant that teamwork was a requirement for students to succeed.

Table 2.1 provides an outline of the sequence of lessons and events the teacher prepared for the students. This case study is an example of how performance assessment, i.e., students 'doing' teamwork, can be used effectively to provide multiple opportunities for students to learn, practise, do, reflect and then learn, practise and do again.

The teacher used an assessment framework that had been co-designed by teachers, students and industry partners to break down the skills and understandings required for teamwork with students. The teacher referred to this framework as "a very live document" where students had "scribbled all over it" as they mapped and tracked their strengths and targeted specific areas. One big shift in the learning design in adopting this approach was for students to

Table 2.1 Planning outline for sequence of lessons

Trip 1 Planning Lesson 1	Introduction PowerPoint
	Sharing of Teamwork Framework
	Group planning Task:
	Students will work in groups of four
	There are four planning stations
	Each group will have ten minutes to contribute via a
	  brainstorm at each planning station (40 minutes)
	Following the brainstorm, the station where you end up
	  becomes your group's station. You will now need to finalise
	  a document that covers all the information required. You
	  will then need to share this with your teacher.
	The stations are:
	  1 Food
	  2 Itinerary and activities
	  3 Packing
	  4 Memories and capturing/documenting the trip

Trip 1 Planning Lesson 2	Working in your planning group, finalise and share the finished product of your topic. You may need to seek feedback from other groups Present your finished planning piece to the group

Trip 1	Throughout this trip there will be many opportunities to
	  demonstrate and utilise your teamwork competencies. In
	  our trip briefing, identify and discus what these might be.

Trip 1 Reflect Lesson	On your copy of the framework, complete the
	  following:
	  • Highlight key items that you feel that you achieved
	    either on the trip or in planning for the trip
	  • Explain with a specific example from the trip, how
	    you achieved this
	  • Write down a goal for the second trip based on your
	    reflections from Trip 1 and identify a personal area of
	    focus for you

Trip 2 Planning Lesson 1	Based on the team reflections from Trip 1, create the
	  following plans
	  • Food – what is changing
	  • Packing List
	  • Tent groupings
	  • Activities

Trip 2 Planning Lesson 2	Trip briefing with activity information shared Question and answer Group share of planning documentation

Trip 2	Throughout this trip, there will be many opportunities to
	  demonstrate and utilise your teamwork competencies. In
	  our trip briefing, identify and discuss what these might be.

Trip 2 Reflect Lesson	Revisit your Teamwork framework Did you achieve your goal? What competencies did you demonstrate on this trip? Provide evidence.

take charge of their learning throughout planning the trips. Previously, there was much more direction with students being told what to do.

Having multiple opportunities to teach, learn, practise and assess a competency such as teamwork, that is usually observed in the moment, was important to build into the planning. It allowed the teacher to observe students over time and minimised concerns about not being able to notice everything. It also allowed students to revisit their learning and to set targeted goals to extend their development. The framework provided students with a structure and language to describe their developing skills that are often referred to in generalities. The teacher ensured that the skills were grounded in context-specific examples that were identified by both the teacher and students as they worked through self-assessment and goal-setting activities.

The experiences of both the teacher and the students in this case study were extremely positive. The teacher noted that the explicit nature of the frameworks enables students to identify what they needed to do in order to improve, and the positive response from the students to this type of assessment even though they were initially surprised by the approach.

> …the students actually see the benefit of it and it's a relief that it's not just around marks on a test and that kind of thing. So, I think that has helped channel my assessment because the students are buying into it.
>
> (Teacher, focus group, 2023)

The students also commented on the benefits of having the skills of teamwork broken down into manageable parts:

> it kind of showed you what a good member of a team does on a trip and it kind of makes you look at your behaviour and not – not like exam – I know the word for it but it made me pay more attention to your behaviour and you thought on the rubric it said this so I'm going to try and be more of that.
>
> (Year 10 student, focus group, 2023)

Adopting this new approach to assessment meant adjusting both the 'what' and the 'how'. The learning and assessment design had to be reimagined using a different lens. This was challenging for both teachers and students at the beginning. Experienced teachers have almost a 'default' way of working, established over years of mastering their craft. We know that any change to entrenched practices requires effort and time. Time to rethink, reorganise and adjust pedagogical practices that are practically implicit. The disruption of introducing a new approach such as this requires support, and built-in mechanisms to provide this support, such as regular meetings to troubleshoot issues and questions around implementation issues. Making these changes when it is not yet a whole-school approach, as it was in this case, also presented challenges with competing priorities. This is where the regular meetings, scheduled during professional learning time, helped this teacher remain focused on the competency-based learning and assessment, rather than it being shuffled down the list of priorities.

Chapter summary and reflection

This chapter discussed the importance of alignment in learning and assessment design. A focus on the construct, knowing the skills, understandings, knowledge, etc. is frontloaded through clear identification of learning objectives. The approach to assessment design relies on knowing the behaviours that demonstrate the learning objectives and then designing appropriate tasks that will provide quality evidence. Transfer is possible but requires explicit teaching. Competency-based assessment requires a mindset shift where the process is as important, if not more important, than the product of assessment.

To help consolidate and consider how what you have read in Chapter 2 connects to your practice, reflect on the following questions:

1 How do the principles of learning and assessment design discussed in this chapter align with your current planning practices?
2 Can you identify any gaps or areas for improvement in your own or others' learning and assessment practices based on the strategies outlined in this chapter?
3 What are some specific action steps you can take to implement one or more of the chapter's recommendations in your teaching or learning context?

Notes

1 Koper, R. (2006). Current research in learning design. *Journal of Educational Technology & Society*, *9*(1), 13–22.
2 Ibid.
3 Biggs, J. (1999). What the student does: Teaching for enhanced learning. *Higher Education Research & Development*, *18*(1), 57–75.
4 Wiggins, G., & McTighe, J. (2005). *Understanding by Design*. Association for Supervision & Curriculum Development.
5 Ibid.
6 Anderson, L.W., & Krathwohl, D.R. (2001). *A taxonomy for learning, teaching, and assessing: A revision of Bloom's taxonomy of educational objectives: Complete edition*. Addison Wesley Longman, Inc.
7 Biggs, J.B., & Collis, K.F. (2014). *Evaluating the quality of learning: The SOLO taxonomy (Structure of the Observed Learning Outcome)*. Academic Press.
8 https://deep-learning.global/.
9 https://curriculumredesign.org/.
10 https://education.unimelb.edu.au/melbourne-assessment/our-research/new-metrics.
11 https://search.oecd.org/education/2030-project/teaching-and-learning/learning/transformative-competencies/Transformative_Competencies_for_2030_concept_note.pdf.

12 Carter, D., & Buchanan, J. (2022). Implementing the general capabilities in New South Wales government primary schools. *Curriculum Perspectives, 42*(2), 145–156.

13 Wiggins, G., & McTighe, J. (2005). *Understanding by Design.* Association for Supervision & Curriculum Development.

14 Clarke, S. (2021). *Unlocking learning intentions and success criteria: Shifting from product to process across the disciplines.* Corwin Press.

15 Perkins, D.N., & Salomon, G. (1989). Are cognitive skills context-bound? *Educational Researcher, 18*(1), 16–25.

16 Perkins, D.N., & Salomon, G. (1992). Transfer of learning. *International Encyclopedia of Education, 2,* 6452–6457.

17 Ibid.

18 Perkins, D.N., & Salomon, G. (2018). *Transfer and teaching thinking. Thinking: The second international conference.* Routledge.

19 Fullan, M., Quinn, J., & McEachen, J. (2017). *Deep learning: Engage the world change the world.* Corwin Press.

20 Perkins, D.N., & Salomon, G. (2018). *Transfer and teaching thinking. Thinking: The second international conference.* Routledge.

21 Cowan, J. (2006). *On Becoming an innovative university teacher: Reflection in action.* McGraw-Hill Education. http://ebookcentral.proquest.com/lib/latrobe/detail.action?docID=287851.

22 Mislevy, R.J., Almond, R.G., & Lukas, J.F. (2003). A brief introduction to evidence-centered design. *ETS Research Report Series, 2003*(1), i–29.

23 Victorian Curriculum and Assessment Authority. (n.d.). *VCAL assessment.* https://www.vcaa.vic.edu.au/assessment/vcal-assessment/Pages/Index.aspx.

24 Miller, G.E. (1990). The assessment of clinical skills/competence/performance. *Academic Medicine, 65*(9), S63–S67.

25 Ibid.

26 https://www2.education.vic.gov.au/pal/reporting-student-achievement/policy.

27 https://educationstandards.nsw.edu.au/wps/portal/nesa/k-10/understanding-the-curriculum/awarding-grades/common-grade-scale.

28 https://www.qcaa.qld.edu.au/downloads/p_10/guidelines_for_reporting_qcar.pdf.

3 Designing assessment tasks

It is planning day for the Year 3/4 teaching and you and your colleagues are meeting to prepare the units of work for Term 2. You pull out the term planner and as per the assessment schedule for the school, Week 5 is typically filled with assessments, mostly standardised tests, that will be used to track cohorts and to inform report writing.

As the planning gets underway, the team identifies a range of tests that are needed for the maths topics, both pre- and post-tests. Diagnostic writing activities and summative writing tasks are scheduled and the Integrated Curriculum History-focused unit is fleshed out. The unit uses an inquiry approach to learning about Explorers.

The teachers at the nearby secondary school are undertaking similar processes in preparation for Term 2. Meeting as a Humanities and Social Sciences (HASS) discipline-based team teaching the Year 8s, they review the unit on Rainforests. There are two assessment tasks for this unit, a fieldwork booklet to be completed in conjunction with an excursion to a local rainforest, and an end-of-unit test. Results will be shared through the school's continuous reporting platform.

Types of assessment tasks

Any task can be considered an assessment task if it is used to elicit evidence of learning. We can categorise assessment tasks in various ways, formative or summative, test or performance, informal or formal. We build in informal assessments all the time as we question, observe and make adjustments during a lesson. Some of these are intentionally planned while others occur on the spot in response to our observations.

Formal assessments are more controlled and typically have set conditions for administering the tasks. This may be the time allowed for the task, seating arrangements, time for planning, reviewing and editing, etc. But before diving deeper into different types of assessments, there are some other ways of thinking about assessment tasks that are worthwhile considering.

DOI: 10.4324/9781032657219-3

Authentic versus meaningful

Authentic assessment tasks are recognised for promoting learning given the robust way they reflect the construct and the positive impact they have on learners.[1] Given the rise of generative AI technology, authentic assessment is now also being seen as a way of protecting tasks against misuse. But what does 'authentic assessment' mean? Ask a colleague next time you see them about how they define authentic in this case.

Using the term, 'authentic assessment' can be problematic as there is no consensus about what this means. In some instances, authentic assessment is used synonymously with performance assessment, in others a distinction is made.[2] Even the characteristics of authentic assessment vary from author to author, with various models put forward. One model that has a lot of traction is the five-dimensional framework of authentic assessment[3] that identifies the assessments task, the physical context, the social context, the assessment result or form, and the assessment criteria as aspects of assessment that are variable in terms of their authenticity. The most notable aspect of this approach to authentic assessment is that of student perspectives and perceived relevance. For a task to be considered authentic, students should have a sense of ownership over the task and see it as "representative, relevant, and meaningful"[4] (p. 71). When we design authentic assessments, we often focus on the degree to which the task replicates a 'real-world' experience or requirement in the discipline. We don't often stop to consider whether the students find it meaningful or representative, beyond the grade they receive on their report for completing the task.

So not only is there a debate about what we mean by authentic assessment, but we can now add the question of 'authentic for whom?' The more we consider authenticity, the more questions come to the surface, like:

- Who decides what is authentic?
- What are the characteristics that make it authentic?
- Is it authentic if students don't recognise authenticity?
- What is the role of the learner in 'authentic assessment'? What agency do they have?
- How is performance in authentic assessments measured? Are these measures 'authentic'?
- Should all tasks be authentic?

We suggest that a more useful approach to framing 'authentic assessment' is to explore what constitutes meaningful assessment. Meaningful assessment

- aligns with learning,
- connects to purpose,
- connects to student interests and goals,

- allows for student agency and choice,
- connects to complex competencies (e.g., collaboration, communication, critical thinking),
- employs useful measures (i.e., the measurement tool or assessment task is reliable and valid).

Assessment should be meaningful for all stakeholders with clear and transparent processes shared and understood by teachers, students and caregivers alike. In place of the oft-used 'disposable' assessments that are employed, a move to non-disposable and more meaningful assessment has the potential to increase learner engagement motivation and ultimately performance.

Disposable versus non-disposable assessment tasks

Many teachers upon returning corrected assessment activities to students will no doubt have been asked the question, "What do I do with this? Can I just put it in the bin?" This is an awkward question from students and our usual suggestion was for them to take it home, share it with their family, use it for review, etc. Ultimately, we knew the piece was likely ending up in the bin either on the way out of the classroom door or the bin at home. This type of assessment task can be described as **disposable**. The work students generate to demonstrate their learning is limited to the student-teacher dyad. In other words, the student completes the work, the teacher marks it and hands it back, and the student puts it in the bin.

Non-disposable assessments on the other hand go beyond the student-teacher exchange. They add value to the world in some way.[5] The degree of this depends on the nature of the task itself, with the potential to extend into the local community and beyond. They require collaboration and exchange of information as students demonstrate and draw on the targeted competencies to complete a task for which their efforts will be recognised beyond the mark book.

At a time when generative AI models are challenging traditional approaches to assessments, non-disposable assessments can provide a meaningful alternative that provides students with ways of demonstrating the learning objectives. They provide higher levels of engagement and motivation as students are able to find more purpose, meaning, autonomy and value in a task that asks for more than answering test questions or writing an essay.[6] Assessment is no doubt a motivating factor that shapes the way students engage with a task, particularly amongst secondary school students. One of the first questions asked is whether the task will be assessed for summative purposes, or plainly put, 'Will the result for this end up on my report?' However, to achieve an accurate representation of students' development levels, it is essential that their motivation to engage extends beyond just summative tasks.

Non-disposable assessments include products that are shared with:[7]

- The general public (e.g., open resources such as an online books)
- Stakeholders (e.g., shared with school leadership, parent community, wider community, government agencies, organisations)
- The school community (e.g., year level, whole school, parents)
- Classmates (e.g., class presentations, peer-reviewed work)

Types of tasks include:

- Publishing a physical or electronic book that is housed in the school library and can be borrowed by others
- Debates
- Performances and screenings
- Exhibited work
- Design-thinking projects that target an identified local issue
- Websites
- Student conferences
- TED talks

As with all decisions regarding learning and assessment design, it is important to have a balance of tasks. It may not always be appropriate for your setting to only offer non-disposable tasks. But it is an important consideration to think about the ways in which teachers and students engage in assessments and create conditions that will engage and motivate learners beyond what appears on their school report.

Nested versus stand-alone assessment tasks

Another way of thinking about assessment tasks is whether they are **stand-alone** or **nested**. Nested assessment tasks, also referred to as staged assessment tasks, provide a built-in mechanism for ensuring that students have multiple opportunities to learn, practice and demonstrate the intended learning outcomes. A nested assessment approach is where different components or layers of assessment tasks are interconnected, building upon each other to develop students' understanding and application of the intended learning outcomes. For example, a larger project may be broken down into three or more smaller parts, where students receive feedback on each part, before moving on to the next.

Because the nature of the skills in each component will be repeated, students can reflect on their learning, and identify areas to address in the next layer of the assessment. The foundational skills required for the first task will become more complex as students develop their skills and understanding of the construct and can apply their developing skills to increasingly complex stages.

As these 'parts' act as formative tasks, students are supported in their development with opportunities to apply the feedback. We often teach in discrete units and in our endeavours to cover the curriculum, the message to students that learning is cumulative and development occurs over time, can be lost. Nested assessments emphasise this concept, making it engaging for students by clearly showing the significance of each component. As students progress through the sequence, they can readily see how each part builds upon the previous one, allowing them to apply their skills and understandings effectively.

Stand-alone assessment tasks on the other hand are discrete tasks that are designed to capture the evidence of learning within that task. There may be connections between other assessments in the unit or topic, but they may or may not reflect the same skills, understanding, etc.

As highlighted in Chapter 2, learning and assessment design must go hand-in-hand. Nested assessments demand this as careful planning and design are required to ensure that each task meaningfully contributes to the overall intended learning outcomes. They require having sufficient time to space the assessments to provide feedback to learners. When implemented appropriately, nested assessments complement what we know about effective cognitive learning and the importance of making connections to prior knowledge and the development and shaping of schemas.

Examples of nested assessments for primary and secondary students are described in Box 3.1. The first example, designed for Years 3 and 4, provides opportunities for students to engage with the concepts in various ways, from initial research to hands-on application culminating with reflection and presentation. It provides multiple means of action and expression as well as representation or ways in which students can engage with and demonstrate what they know and can do (see Universal Design for Learning discussion in Chapter 4) and encourages critical thinking and problem-solving. The connection to real-world experiences creates a more engaging and meaningful experience. The secondary school example focuses on Geography and illustrates how a nested assessment can target not only factual knowledge but also a range of competencies including critical thinking, technical skills, problem-solving and communication.

Box 3.1   Example of nested assessment

Primary

Year level: 3/4
   Topic: Plant life cycles (Australian Curriculum content description ACSSU072)
   Intended learning outcome: Students will understand the stages of a plant's life cycle and factors affecting plant growth.
   Diagnostic assessment: Students complete an activity responding to images and questions about plant life cycles. This is supplemented with a concept map using key terms from a provided list. Adjustments

to the task (e.g., content, process, product) are based on students' existing prior knowledge.

Stage 1: Research and Diagram Drawing (Understanding and Knowledge)

Task: Students start by researching the life cycle of a common plant (e.g., a bean plant). They use books and online resources (with guidance) to gather information about each stage of the cycle: germination, growth, flowering, pollination, seed formation and seed dispersal.

Outcome: Students create a detailed diagram of the plant's life cycle, labelling each stage and providing a short description.

Assesses: Ability to collect and understand relevant information.

Stage 2: Growth Experiment (Application and Analysis)

Task: Building on their knowledge from Stage 1, students plant their beans in small pots. They design an experiment to observe how different conditions (e.g., amount of sunlight and water) affect the plant's growth. This requires predicting outcomes, recording observations and making adjustments.

Outcome: Students keep a journal of their observations, including measurements and photos over time, to document the growth process and the effects of each variable.

Assesses: Ability to apply knowledge in a practical context and analyse data.

Stage 3: Presentation and Reflection (Synthesis and Evaluation)

Task: Using the information from their diagrams and the results of their growth experiment, students create a presentation. The presentation will explain the plant life cycle, experimental design, observations and conclusions about the factors affecting plant growth.

Outcome: Students present their findings to the class, demonstrating their understanding and ability to communicate scientific concepts. They also reflect on what they learned, what surprised them, and what they might do differently in future experiments.

Assesses: Ability to synthesise and evaluate information, as well as reflect on their learning process.

Secondary

Year level: 8

  Unit 1: Landforms and landscapes

  Intended learning outcome: Students will understand how natural features and human activities influence each other and shape the geographic characteristics of different places.

Diagnostic assessment: Students are given a list of key terms related to the unit (e.g., topography, climate, urbanisation and sustainable development) and asked to create a concept map. This map should link these terms in ways that reflect the student's current understanding of how they interrelate. Adjustments to the task (e.g., content, process and product) are based on students' existing prior knowledge.

Phase 1: Research and Analysis

Task 1: Comparative Study – Students select two distinct geographic locations (e.g., a coastal city and a mountainous region). They research both areas focusing on natural characteristics (climate, topography, flora and fauna) and human aspects (population, land use and urban planning). The goal is to understand how each area's natural environment influences human settlement and activity, and vice versa.

Task 2: Impact Report – Based on their comparative study, students write a detailed report on a specific environmental or human process (such as urbanisation, deforestation, climate change or sustainable development practices) in their chosen locations. They analyse how these processes have altered the geographic characteristics of these places over time.

Phase 2: Application and Presentation

Task 3: GIS Mapping Project – Using Geographic Information Systems (GIS) tools, students create interactive maps that visualise data related to their research (e.g., population density, land use changes, deforestation rates). This task assesses students' ability to use technology to represent geographic data and trends visually.

Task 4: Solutions and Strategies Presentation – Students develop a presentation proposing solutions or strategies to mitigate negative impacts identified in their impact report, focusing on sustainability and environmental conservation. This could involve urban planning initiatives, conservation efforts or community-based strategies. They present their findings and proposals to the class, encouraging discussion on the feasibility and potential impacts of these solutions.

Phase 3: Reflection and Synthesis

Task 5: Reflective Essay – Students write a reflective essay on what they learned about the interplay between environmental and human processes in shaping places and environments. They reflect on the importance of sustainable practices and how geographic knowledge can contribute to resolving environmental challenges.

Task 6: Peer Review – As a final step, students participate in a peer review session, providing constructive feedback on each other's presentations and proposed solutions. This encourages critical thinking.

Traditional versus alternative assessment tasks

Traditional assessment tasks refer to conventional methods of measuring students' knowledge and skills through structured formats. These assessments can be characterised by the standardised ways in which they are administered and scored. Typically, traditional assessments aim to measure students' proficiency in specific areas of learning by evaluating how well they recall, understand and apply information, with a reliance on tests.[8]

Alternative assessments, on the other hand, are tasks that are designed to replicate the ways in which the skills, knowledge and understanding are actually applied. They are designed to be more integrative and comprehensive, focusing on students' ability to apply knowledge in practical or novel situations rather than just recalling facts or demonstrating rote skills.[9] Alternative assessment strategies are process and performance-based and can be considered performance-and-product assessments as both product and performance are simultaneously the target and the means of assessment.[10] Examples of performance tasks include portfolios, role-plays or simulation-based tasks, debates, investigations, etc. The remainder of this chapter will refer to alternative assessment as performance assessment.

Both traditional and performance assessments will be discussed in more detail later in this chapter.

Task complexity and task difficulty

When we design any assessment task, whether that be a test, essay question or performance task, we consider the appropriateness of the items or the task itself. Is it too easy? Is it too hard? The purpose of an assessment task is to provide you with information about what students know and can do, and what they are ready to learn next. If the task is too easy and a student gets everything correct or achieves the highest levels of criteria for each item, we do not learn anything about what they do not know. If a task or item is too hard for a student and they do not get anything correct or are unable to demonstrate the minimum required skills and knowledge, then we also do not learn anything new about the student. These are known as floor and ceiling effects (see also Chapter 2). Students hit the ceiling of a test when they are unable to demonstrate the limits of their current understandings and skills. The floor effect occurs when a test (or any other assessment) is so difficult that students are unable to respond correctly to many, if any, items on a test.

Therefore, determining the appropriate range of items (test questions, essay questions, etc.) to enable the collection of useful evidence of learning is an important consideration. This impacts not just a student's ability to complete the task but also their motivation. We identify two aspects to be considered when designing performance tasks or traditional assessments: complexity and difficulty. These two terms are often conflated and used interchangeably, but they refer to different aspects of the design.

The study of task complexity is widespread, touching on various disciplines such as decision making, goal setting, auditing, human-computer interaction and second language acquisition. There is not a single, universally accepted definition of complexity; however, we define task complexity as "the aggregation of any intrinsic task characteristic that affects task performance" (p. 559).[11] This definition is the cornerstone of an integrated approach to analysing task complexity.

A useful way of thinking about difficulty is through 'effort', where the degree of required effort is subjective to the learner, whereas task complexity is objective[12] and can be considered a design consideration. The continuum for difficulty is anchored by easy versus hard, whereas changes in complexity vary from more to less.

Given the degree of variability in student development in any learning area at any time, it is important to draw on prior knowledge of the student cohort to ensure the task has a difficulty level that will allow for judgements to be made for all learners. A task that is too easy or too hard for some will prove to be a waste of time in many regards as this fails to provide any information or evidence of learning. For traditional assessments, this may mean having a range of items that spread across a range of difficulty. Easy items will see many correct responses, whereas the more difficult items will only be achieved by a few students. If providing a range of items is not practical in terms of length or nature of the task, adjust the assessment for different groups of learners.

Apart from ensuring that assessment tasks yield worthwhile information about student progress, there are some other notable reasons for being cognisant of complexity and difficulty when designing tasks. These relate to students' ability and motivation to engage. The theory of flow, proposed by positive psychologist Mihalyi Csikszentmihalyi, describes a state of focus and engagement that is directly related to the conditions of a task.[13] For optimal 'flow' there needs to be a balance between the individual's skill level and the difficulty of the activity. If the activity is too easy, it can create a state of boredom leading to decreased attention and motivation. If the activity is too hard, it creates a sense of anxiety. This also leads to decreased motivation and can impair performance. This idea is reflected in achievement motivation research that provides a framework for how and why individuals are motivated to engage in certain tasks and achieve specific outcomes.[14] The two main factors are expectancy of success and value. If learners believe they are likely to succeed, they are more motivated to engage in the task. Alternatively, if they do not believe they can succeed (based on previous experience, perceived difficulty, self-efficacy) or their likelihood to succeed is low, their motivation will decrease (see Chapter 4 for more on student engagement). The element of value is subdivided into four types: intrinsic value (inherent interest/enjoyment), utility value (how useful it is for future goals), attainment value (importance of doing well) and cost (potential failure, effort, time to engage).

While these frameworks provide teachers with considerations for individual students and the difficulty of the task, complexity of the task will contribute to individual levels of perceived difficulty and represents deliberate design choices. Drawing on models of complexity and the frameworks discussed above, we identify the following design elements that characterise any assessment activity:

1   Learner agency: includes perceived value and motivation to succeed in the task. Relates to making connections as to the purpose of the task, and the scope for students to make decisions about features of task design (e.g., process, product, content).
2   Process: the number of steps required to complete the task and the degree of structure provided or inherent for each step. This includes whether steps follow a general sequence or require prioritisation of multiple sub-tasks.
3   Familiarity with content/processes: how much prior knowledge is required to successfully complete the task and to what extent this is explicitly taught prior to the task.
4   Support: the degree to which learners are supported or guided through scaffolding or direct input from the teacher.
5   Temporal dynamics and planning: what are the time constraints or timelines (and associated pressures)?

Finding the optimal level of challenge is not an easy task in itself. But by considering aspects of difficulty (easy-hard) and complexity (less-more), assessments can be designed to accommodate all learners to ensure that they have the opportunity to demonstrate what they know and can do and are equally motivated to do so.

Selecting assessment activities

All teachers consider and plan for how they will assess learning at the time of planning, regardless of the age of the learners, or the nature of the learning. And there is a plethora of diagnostic, formative and summative tasks that can be used. Selecting and designing assessment tasks requires consideration of the learning design, as discussed in Chapter 2, and a clearly defined understanding of *what* and *why* they are assessing. In the context of developmental assessment, the focus expands from 'knowing' and 'knowing how' (as per Miller's Model of Clinical Competence discussed in Chapter 2), to include showing and doing. This is in recognition that development in any competency requires application and use of transferable knowledge and skills in any given situation.[15]

A key consideration when planning and designing assessment activities is that the task(s) elicits quality evidence and is used purposefully to ensure validity and reliability. If the 'tool' used to collect the evidence in the first place is flawed, then the judgements we make, and the decisions we make based on the resulting information need to be considered cautiously. The scenario in Box 3.2 illustrates how the tool can negatively impact the learning of students. On the surface, it seems Ms Thompson is serving her students well, using evidence of what students know and are ready to learn next to inform her planning for targeted teaching. Unfortunately, the nature of the test compromised the quality of the evidence she was basing this on.

Box 3.2   Scenario

In a Year 7 mathematics classroom, Ms Thompson has just introduced a unit on algebraic expressions. To assess her students' understanding, she decides to administer a written test that includes a mix of multiple-choice questions, short answer problems and a longer problem-solving task.

The issue arises with the longer problem-solving task, where students are asked to create and solve an algebraic equation based on a real-life scenario involving a train journey. The scenario involves complex language and concepts that Ms Thompson had not explicitly covered in her lessons. Unfortunately, the task proves to be confusing for many students, leading to varied and inconsistent responses.

Several students struggle to understand the scenario and their attempts to create algebraic equations show significant misunderstandings. Some students misinterpret the wording, while others attempt to use incorrect mathematical operations. As a result, the evidence gathered from this particular task is not a valid representation of the students' grasp of algebraic concepts.

However, unaware of the validity issues in the assessment, Ms Thompson proceeds to use the collected data to make decisions about the next steps in her teaching. She identifies a group of students who, based on their performance in the problematic task, seem to require additional support. Ms Thompson decides to spend extra class time reviewing the concepts covered in the assessment, assuming that the difficulties arise from a lack of understanding rather than the flawed nature of the task.

In the following weeks, Ms Thompson focuses her teaching on reiterating the algebraic concepts related to the train journey scenario. She uses additional practice problems and provides supplementary materials to support the struggling students. Unfortunately, because the original assessment task was invalid, Ms Thompson's efforts to address the students' needs may not be as effective as intended.

As a consequence, the students may continue to experience challenges in algebra, leading to potential gaps in their understanding that could persist into future units.

Regardless of whether the task used is a traditional test format, or a nested performance task, teaching teams need to take the time to review the task prior to administering assessments with cohorts of students. A checklist is provided in Box 3.3 to assist in evaluating assessment tasks. While the checklist looks long, it is likely that most of these factors have implicitly been considered in the design. Using a checklist such as this will ensure that you can review assessments, both your own and those created by others, objectively.

Box 3.3   Checklist for evaluating assessment tasks

Evaluating assessment tasks is crucial to ensure they effectively measure the intended learning outcomes and provide valuable insights into students' learning. Consider the following factors when selecting assessment tasks.

Alignment with intended learning outcomes

- Does the assessment align with the stated learning objectives or outcomes?
- Have the students had an opportunity to learn and practice what is being assessed?
- Is there a clear connection between what is being assessed and what students are expected to learn?

Validity

- Does the assessment measure what it intends to measure?
- Are the questions/tasks representative of the content and skills covered in the unit?

Reliability

- Are the assessment tasks consistent in measuring student performance over time?
- Have the tasks been piloted or tested for reliability?

Clarity and transparency

- Are the instructions for the assessment clear and easy to understand?
- Is the grading criteria explicit and transparent to both students and assessors?

Fairness and ethical considerations

- Are there potential biases in the assessment that may disadvantage certain groups of students?
- Are there options provided for students with diverse learning needs (e.g., additional planning time, technology support or a modified task)?
- Are there any ethical concerns associated with the assessment?
- Have you considered the potential impact on students' well-being and mental health?

Meaningful

- Does the assessment reflect real-world tasks or scenarios that students might encounter in contexts beyond the classroom?
- Are the tasks meaningful and relevant to the students?

Practicality

- Is the assessment feasible in terms of time, resources and logistics?
- Can it be administered and graded efficiently?

Variety of assessment methods

- Does the assessment use a variety of methods (e.g., exams, projects or presentations) to capture different aspects of learning?
- Are there both formative and summative assessment components?

Feedback opportunities

- Does the assessment provide opportunities for timely and constructive feedback?
- Can students learn from the assessment experience to improve future performance?

Technology integration

- If applicable, does the assessment leverage technology appropriately?
- What are the possibilities for the use and misuse of generative AI?

Engagement and motivation

- Will the assessment tasks engage and motivate students to put forth their best effort?
- Are the tasks interesting and relevant to the students' experiences and interests?

Reflection

- Have you considered including reflective elements in the assessment, allowing students to assess their own learning?
- Are there opportunities for peer feedback?

Performance tasks

Performance-based assessments are valuable for both summative and formative purposes and are seen as more effective than standardised tests in capturing more complex performances and processes.[16] Performance-based assessments allow the assessment of students over a period of time using a wide range of tasks and the reliability of teachers' judgements are comparable to those of standardised tests.[17] Performance assessment can be defined as

> a structured situation in which stimulus materials and a request for information or action are presented to an individual, who generates a response that can be rated for quality using explicit standards. The standards may apply to the final product or the process of creating it.[18]
>
> (p. 21)

This is different to a multiple-choice test where students make a selection. They are typically complex, concrete tasks that can be further characterised by:

1 The way learners engage or respond to the elements of the task (questions),
2 The type of response expected from the learner (products or outputs),
3 The ways in which the responses are scored,
4 The degree to which they reflect real-world scenarios,
5 The use of linked sub-tasks that potentially lead to a final, comprehensive task.[19]

See Box 3.4 for a selection of possible performance tasks.

Box 3.4   Types of performance tasks

Portfolios

Curated collections of students' work showcasing their efforts, progress and achievements in one or more areas. They can include a variety of materials such as written assignments, projects, photographs and reflections, offering a comprehensive view of a student's development over time.

Presentations

Students prepare and deliver a presentation on a specific topic, demonstrating their understanding, research skills and ability to communicate effectively. Presentations can be individual or group projects.

Projects

Project-based assessments require students to apply their knowledge and skills to complete a comprehensive project. This could involve research projects, science experiments, design thinking projects, video productions and artwork.

Performances

In Arts-based learning areas or Physical Education, students may be assessed based on their performance in activities such as drama, music performances, dance routines or athletic or game-based skills.

Simulations and role-plays

Simulations and role-plays involve creating realistic scenarios that students must navigate and apply their knowledge in practical settings.

Written assignments

Written assignments, including essays, research papers and journals, require students to articulate their ideas, conduct research, etc. Though traditional in format, these assessments can be performance-based if they require application of skills in analysis, synthesis and evaluation.

The extended nature of performance tasks provides students and teachers with multiple opportunities to demonstrate and observe development in the targeted construct by focusing on the processes students employ as they work towards the final product. They go beyond the knowing and knowing how in Miller's model of clinical competence to demonstrate students' ability to show and do. This not only increases the reliability of the assessment and subsequent judgements, but also provides valuable information for targeted teaching. When students are provided with multiple opportunities to show their current level of performance, teachers are able to intervene and provide the necessary teaching to support further development and create opportunities for transfer.

Planning for performance tasks is no different in many respects to planning for traditional assessment and comes back to the points raised in Chapter 2. There must be clarity about what is being assessed and this is guided by the learning objectives and the underlying constructs (knowledge, understandings) that are the focus of the learning design. It is crucial to understand which behaviours indicate that the learning objectives have been met and how these behaviors will be measured. The task should provide quality evidence that is current, authentic (the work of the student), appropriate, sufficient and consistent. Be on the lookout for elements of the task that may prove to be barriers or assess something else that will compromise the quality of the evidence.

Considerations when planning performance assessments

There are a number of things to consider from the outset when planning performance assessments. These include aspects related to complexity of the task (number of steps, duration, scaffolding, etc.), scoring and the unit of analysis (typically the individual student). Providing all students with the same task and the same support may prove problematic as there will be variation in the degree of support required based on the complexity of the task. Planning for ways in which students need to be supported from the beginning is essential to student engagement with the task. When the assessment focus is on the construct then it becomes easier to consider different ways students can demonstrate those skills and understandings. In other words, if the construct is being demonstrated, do the conditions have to be exactly the same for everyone? (see Chapter 5 for more on this topic).

Scoring for performance assessments is not as black and white as for traditional methods where there is typically a right and wrong response. Given the complex skills and nature of the tasks, the risk of inconsistent judgements and subjective decisions across markers is high. Developing robust assessment frameworks, like developmental rubrics, is a key strategy to protect against this. Checklists and rating scales are also options. Scoring and interpretation using rubrics will be unpacked in Chapter 5.

The unit of analysis for almost all assessment in school or educational settings is the individual. We assess and report on what the individual learner can do. Interestingly, outside of the school context, very little of the work we do is achieved as an individual. Rather, our efforts are collaborative to some degree. The design of performance tasks can often involve group work, creating a challenge for teachers as they try to separate individual contributions to a group task. I'm sure we all have our own frustrations about working in a group with team members who may not contribute but reap the same rewards! This doesn't mean we avoid this, rather we can draw on relevant curriculum and build it into the assessment framework such as the Social Management element of Personal and Social Capability (Australian Curriculum).

A strategy that we have found useful when designing and planning for performance assessments is to consult with a small group of students to get their feedback on the planned task and scoring method. Providing past, current or future students (or a combination) with the task and scoring guide and asking for their suggestions has proved valuable in ensuring the task is clearly explained and matched to the assessment criteria.

Traditional assessment: Tests

As discussed earlier in this chapter, traditional assessments typically refer to tests. Tests come in many forms: standardised/non-standardised, high or low stakes, short answer or multiple choice. We often think of tests requiring pen and paper, completed independently in (often timed) conditions that ensure it is the students' own work. This means working in silence at separate desks, or perhaps with clipboards or exercise books set up as barriers to ameliorate the risk of wandering eyes and copying answers.

Tests have been a staple of school-based assessment practices beginning in the early years of schooling and culminating in the high-stakes exams that form part of a senior secondary certificate for many students. Testing is largely used for diagnostic and summative purposes. But tests can also be used to promote learning[20] in what is known as the testing effect. The testing effect refers to the memory gains that can help improve learning and retention for later testing. The key lies in the use of regular testing, such as weekly quizzes on the material learnt that week. A study with college students found that quizzing improved learning student achievement and that using short answer weekly quizzes improved performance more so than weekly multiple-choice quizzes.[21]

Tests can be used to assess a variety of types of understandings and knowledge,[22] including:

- Factual knowledge: the ability to recall and apply facts and information. For example, musical symbols and historical events.
- Conceptual knowledge: the ability to understand the way the different parts of a complex system interact and depend on each other to function properly. For example, Pythagorus' theorem and plate tectonics.
- Procedural knowledge: the ability to understand and carry out a sequence of steps to complete a task including methods of inquiry, techniques, algorithms, etc. For example, scientific method and solving a maths problem.
- Metacognitive knowledge: the ability to draw on general strategies for different tasks, as well as using knowledge of self as a learner. For example, knowing one's own strengths and weakness and planning strategies.

No single test type can assess all of these types of understandings. Different types of tests are better suited for assessing different types of understanding. Some test types, like multiple choice and true/false tests, only require recognition, others such as short answer or essay responses require recall. In general, recall tests are more difficult than recognition tests. This is because recall tests require students to actively retrieve information from memory, while recognition tests only require students to identify information that they have previously seen or heard. Recall tests are also more effective at promoting long-term learning than recognition tests.[23] This is because the process of retrieving information from memory strengthens the neural connections associated with that information.

When developing or selecting a test, teachers should carefully consider the type of knowledge that they want to assess and choose the type of test that is most appropriate. For example, if the teacher wants to assess students' conceptual understanding of a topic, then they might use an essay test or a short answer test. If the teacher wants to assess students' factual knowledge of a topic, then they might use a multiple-choice test or a true/false test. Table 3.1 summarises the types of knowledge and associated tests for use with students.

Standardised versus non-standardised tests

Both standardised and non-standardised tests are commonly used in classrooms. The biggest difference between them is that standardised tests are published with a set of uniform, or 'standard', administrative instructions to ameliorate the amount of noise in the data and allow for comparison. For example, the commonly used Progressive Achievement Tests (PAT) suite from the Australian Council of Educational Research (ACER) provides scale scores that allow for multiple points of comparison and tracking of student progress.[24]

Student performance on a test needs to be interpreted and compared in some way, and this is known as 'referencing'. It involves comparing a student's performance on a test to a specific reference group or a predetermined standard. This comparison helps to understand how well a test-taker

Table 3.1 Types of knowledge and associated tests for use with students

Type of knowledge	What is required of student	Types of tests best suited
Factual	Students recall specific facts and information	Multiple choice True/False Matching Fill-in-the blank
Conceptual	Students apply knowledge of classifications, categories, to new situations to demonstrate understanding of concepts, generalisations, theories etc.	Essays Short answer Problem-solving
Procedural	Students demonstrate understanding of sequence of steps to complete a task	Performance tasks Multi-step problems
Metacognitive	Students demonstrate self-awareness and require engagement with learning process	Best assessed via classroom activities/discussions Reflective essays Interviews

performed in relation to others or against a predefined criterion. There are two main types of referencing in educational testing: **norm-referenced** and **criterion-referenced**.

Norm-referenced testing

Norm-referenced testing involves comparing an individual's performance to the performance of a group of people, often referred to as the norming or reference group. This type of testing provides information about how a student's performance ranks in comparison to the performance of a larger population. These norms are regularly updated and are established using the results of a sample that represents the diversity within the population. For example, the PAT Maths and Reading norms were updated in 2022 using results data from nearly 2 million tests.[25] Norm-referenced tests are often used to rank and compare students. For example, if a student takes a norm-referenced standardised test and scores in the 75th percentile, it means they performed better than 75% of the norming group (typically based on age). They help identify relative strengths and weaknesses among test takers but do not necessarily provide information about the absolute level of knowledge or skill.[26]

Criterion-referenced testing

Criterion-referenced testing involves comparing an individual's performance against a specific set of criteria or standards, rather than against the performance of a group. The focus is on determining whether the student has mastered a particular set of skills or knowledge that are aligned with the predefined learning objectives. For example, in a criterion-referenced test, a student will be assessed based on their actual performance across the skills or knowledge providing insight into areas of strength and weakness. Criterion-referenced tests are designed to measure a test taker's absolute level of performance against predetermined standards. They are often used to assess mastery of specific skills or knowledge.

Non-standardised tests are those that come without the uniform set of procedures and are often developed in-house by teachers, either individually or a team. The test may consist of items drawn from various textbooks or items created by the teacher for the specific test. These types of tests are commonly called teacher-made tests (TMT). As with any achievement test, reliability and validity are important, particularly content validity.[27] Writing tests is a difficult task that takes time. Whether it be an essay question, short answer or multiple-choice questions, there are steps that teachers can take to increase validity and meaningfulness of student results.

What makes a good test?

A test needs to allow students opportunity to demonstrate what they know and can do without additional barriers getting in the way, such as reading comprehension levels interfering with understanding a mathematical problem or time management compromising results in a timed test. Other barriers such as cultural background or gender can also have an impact. This was evident when the National Assessment Program Literacy and Numeracy (NAPLAN) was adapted to a local context by the NSW Aboriginal and Education Consultative Group that resulted in improvements in reading scores for indigenous and non-indigenous students.[28] These types of adaptions won't be possible with many standardised tests; however, for TMT this should be a key consideration.

A good test is an effective test, a test that serves its purpose. Knowing the purpose seems obvious, but we recall conversations with primary teaching colleagues where the reason for administering weekly spelling tests was unknown to the teaching team. This is not necessarily uncommon. As teachers, we can get stuck in a routine of assessment without giving the purpose of the assessment much consideration. Of course, the procedural steps outlined in Chapter 2 address this, but when creating tests, we can use a table of specifications, or a test blueprint, to ensure that we remain focused on the competencies we want to assess.

Test blueprints

A test blueprint, also known as a table of specifications, is a matrix that is a useful starting point for designing a test that improves the quality of the test and, therefore, the evidence of student achievement.[29] It acts as a roadmap, as any blueprint does, outlining both the structure and the content of the assessment. As discussed in Chapter 2, alignment between learning and assessment design is essential and the blueprint provides a form of accountability that can be used to ensure the learning outcomes are being addressed. This may seem obvious, but throughout our teaching careers, we have certainly heard students comment that there was content on the test that was not taught, or if it was taught, little time and attention was spent on it.

The structure and organisation of the blueprint can take many forms, depending on the needs and wants of the teachers designing the test. It can be as simple as the example shown in Figure 3.1. This example lists the learning outcomes from the initial planning documents in a row and the columns represent a level of cognitive complexity and type of knowledge (see Table 3.1). Using this matrix, teachers can plan and review the number of questions and/or value of points associated with each learning outcome. A high number of questions appearing in the lower levels of cognitive complexity that require recall or repetition of a process would flag that the test items should be reviewed to increase cognitive demand.

While a simple version of a blueprint can be helpful, by adding in a few extra details, the roadmap can provide a clear picture of the alignment between learning and assessment design. Figure 3.2 shows a more comprehensive blueprint that includes the time spent on the topic and number of test items, and

Bloom's Level / Learning Outcome	Understand	Apply	Create	Totals
Generate equivalent fractions using models	3	2	3	8
Represent fractions on a number line	0	5	5	10
Add fractions with like denominator	5	5	0	10
Multiply fractions by whole numbers	0	5	0	5
Totals	10	20	10	40

Figure 3.1 Simple test blueprint.

Learning Outcome	Time spent on topic (minutes)	Percent of class time on topic	Number of test items	Lower levels • Remember • Understand	Higher levels • Apply • Analyse • Evaluate • Create
Generate equivalent fractions using models	180	30	5	2 Multiple choice	3 short-answer
Represent fractions on a number line	150	25	5	1 Multiple choice	4 short-answer
Add fractions with like denominator	150	25	5	2 T/F	3 short-answer
Multiply fractions by whole numbers	120	20	5	0	5 short-answer
Totals	600	100	25	5	15

Figure 3.2 Sample test blueprint with additional specifications.

identifies the type of question that will be used.[30] The benefit of specifying the time spent on the construct lies in the proportion of the test that should be allocated to that construct. Of course, the practicalities of teaching mean that planned time often does not eventuate to actual time spent learning content due to excursions, illness, curriculum days, public holidays or a last-minute assembly with a special guest. But even with the ever-changing nature of competing demands, the blueprint will inform what should be considered valid and reliable evidence of student learning.

Test construction and generative artificial intelligence (gen AI)

With the ever-expanding capabilities of the gen AI models like ChatGPT, Gemini (Google) and Copilot (Microsoft), it makes sense that teachers are outsourcing tasks such as writing test items to these tools. It is important to ensure that the prompts are appropriate and even more important to review the items. The guidelines to review are the same as construction and can be used as a checklist (see Box 3.3).

Considerations when planning traditional assessments

The main considerations when planning traditional assessments come back to the question of alignment. Do the test items accurately and adequately represent the learning objectives? Consider the difficulty and complexity of the items. Will the items be able to provide you with enough information and will the students be able to engage with the selection of items? Do you have a backup plan if there is evidence of a floor or ceiling effect for any students?

Interpretation of test scores is also an important consideration. If raw scores are simply converted to a percentage, consider the quality and useability of information you and the learner can access from this. Do you accept the score as is, even if it is inconsistent with what you know about the learner? We know that test anxiety leads to lower scores[31,32] so how do we manage this when we rely on tests for our assessment and reporting practices?

There is no doubt the efficiency of tests is appealing when selecting an assessment method. They are Easy to administer, quick to mark, objective and can inform teaching and learning decisions based on the patterns of results. A conversation with any student who has a test coming up also demonstrates how studying patterns increase in the short term lead up to tests. But tests also come with text anxiety for some learners, potential bias in the items disadvantaging some groups,[33] and can be limited in what they are able to assess.

Chapter summary and reflection

This chapter has discussed performance and traditional assessments providing an overview of each. Considerations when planning assessment tasks were introduced including disposable and non-disposable assessment, nested and stand-alone tasks, task complexity and task difficulty. These elements of assessment tasks need to be planned and designed to ensure we are providing students with appropriate opportunities to demonstrate what they know and can do in our search for evidence of learning. At the core of all assessment design is knowing what is being assessed and the behaviours to look for that demonstrate the targeted learning objectives.

In order to reflect on what you have read in Chapter 3 and how this might connect to your practice, consider the following questions:

1 How might the concepts of disposable versus non-disposable assessments influence the design of your assessment tasks?

2 How do you currently record, interpret and use test results for teaching and learning and for reporting? Are there opportunities to review the quality of evidence and make any accommodations where necessary?

3 Review an existing assessment task. How might you adjust the complexity and difficulty of your assessment tasks based on your reflection on students' previous performance and feedback?

Notes

1 Gulikers, J.T., Bastiaens, T.J., & Kirschner, P.A. (2004). A five-dimensional framework for authentic assessment. *Educational Technology Research and Development*, 52(3), 67–86.
2 Frey, B.B., Schmitt, V.L., & Allen, J.P. (2019). Defining authentic classroom assessment. *Practical Assessment, Research, and Evaluation*, 17(1), 2.
3 Gulikers, J.T., Bastiaens, T.J., & Kirschner, P.A. (2004). A five-dimensional framework for authentic assessment. *Educational Technology Research and Development*, 52(3), 67–86.
4 Ibid.
5 Wiley, D. (2013). *What is open pedagogy?* https://opencontent.org/blog/archives/2975.
6 Seraphin, S.B., Grizzell, J.A., Kerr-German, A., Perkins, M.A., Grzanka, P.R., & Hardin, E.E. (2018). A conceptual framework for non-disposable assignments: Inspiring implementation, innovation, and research. *Psychology Learning & Teaching*, 18(1), 84–97. https://doi.org/10.1177/1475725718811711.
7 Ibid.
8 Nasab, F.G. (2015). Alternative versus traditional assessment. *Journal of Applied Linguistics and Language Research*, 2(6), 165–178.
9 Anderson, R.S. (1998). Why talk about different ways to grade? The shift from traditional assessment to alternative assessment. *New Directions for Teaching and Learning*, 74, 5–16.
10 Messick, S. (1994). The interplay of evidence and consequences in the validation of performance assessments. *Educational Researcher*, 23(2), 13–23.
11 Liu, P., & Li, Z. (2012). Task complexity: A review and conceptualization framework. *International Journal of Industrial Ergonomics*, 42(6), 553–568. https://doi.org/10.1016/j.ergon.2012.09.001.
12 Kim, J. (2008). Perceived difficulty as a determinant of Web search performance. *Information Research*, 13(4), 13–14.
13 Csikszentmihalyi, M. (1990). *Flow: The psychology of optimal experience*. Harper & Row.
14 Wigfield, A., & Eccles, J.S. (2000). Expectancy-value theory of achievement motivation. *Contemporary Educational Psychology*, 25(1), 68–81. https://doi.org/10.1006/ceps.1999.1015.
15 Organisation for Economic Co-operation and Development. (2005). *Definition and selection of key competencies: Executive summary*. OECD Publishing.
16 Pepper, D. (2013). KeyCoNet 2013 literature review: Assessment for key competences. *Key Competence Network on School Education (KeyCoNet)*.
17 Ibid.
18 Stecher, B. (2014). Looking back: Performance assessment in an era of standards-based educational accountability. In L. Darling-Hammond & F. Adamson (Eds.), *Beyond the bubble test: How performance assessments support 21st Century learning* (pp. 17–52). Jossey-Bass.
19 Davey, T., Ferrara, S., Shavelson, R., Holland, P., Webb, N., & Wise, L. (2015). Psychometric considerations for the next generation of performance assessment.

Washington, DC: Center for K-12 Assessment & Performance Management, Educational Testing Service, 1–100, Commissioned by: Center for K–12 Assessment & Performance Management at ETS Educational Testing Service, https://www.ets.org/Media/Research/pdf/psychometric_considerations_white_paper.pdf.

20 McDaniel, M.A., Anderson, J.L., Derbish, M.H., & Morrisette, N. (2007). Testing the testing effect in the classroom. *European Journal of Cognitive Psychology*, *19*(4–5), 494–513. https://doi.org/10.1080/09541440701326154.

21 Ibid.

22 Anderson, L.W., & Krathwohl, D.R. (2001). *A taxonomy for learning, teaching, and assessing: A revision of Bloom's taxonomy of educational objectives: Complete edition*. Addison Wesley Longman, Inc.

23 McDaniel, M.A., Anderson, J.L., Derbish, M.H., & Morrisette, N. (2007). Testing the testing effect in the classroom. *European Journal of Cognitive Psychology*, *19*(4–5), 494–513. https://doi.org/10.1080/09541440701326154.

24 Australian Council for Educational Research. (2024). PAT Assessments: *The evidence you need to help students grow*. https://www.acer.org/au/pat/assessments.

25 Australian Council for Educational Research. (2024). PAT Insights: Updated Australian norms improve PAT Maths and PAT Reading achievement comparisons. https://www.acer.org/au/pat/pat-insights/updated-australian-norms.

26 Lok, B., McNaught, C., & Young, K. (2016). Criterion-referenced and norm-referenced assessments: Compatibility and complementarity. *Assessment & Evaluation in Higher Education*, *41*(3), 450–465. https://doi.org/10.1080/02602938.2015.1022136.

27 Notar, C.E., Zuelke, D.C., Wilson, J.D., & Yunker, B.D. (2004). The table of specifications: Insuring accountability in teacher made tests. *Journal of Instructional Psychology*, *31*(2), 115.

28 Dobrescu, L., Holden, R., Motta, A., Piccoli, A., Roberts, P., & Walker, S. (2021). *Cultural context in standardized tests*. Technical report, Discussion paper 2021-08, School of Economics, The University of New South Wales, New South Wales, Australia. Available at http://doi.org/10.2139/ssrn.3983663.

29 Abdellatif, H. (2023). Test results with and without blueprinting: Psychometric analysis using the Rasch model. *Educación Médica*, *24*(3), 100802. https://doi.org/10.1016/j.edumed.2023.100802.

30 Fives, H., & DiDonato-Barnes, N. (2019). Classroom test construction: The power of a table of specifications. *Practical Assessment, Research, and Evaluation*, *18*(1), 3.

31 Cassady, J.C., & Johnson, R.E. (2002). Cognitive test anxiety and academic performance. *Contemporary Educational Psychology*, *27*(2), 270–295.

32 Woldeab, D., & Brothen, T. (2019). 21st century assessment: Online proctoring, test anxiety, and student performance. *International Journal of E-Learning & Distance Education/Revue internationale du e-learning et la formation à distance*, *34*(1). Retrieved from https://www.ijede.ca/index.php/jde/article/view/1106

33 Taylor, C.S. (2022). *Culturally and socially responsible assessment: Theory, research, and practice*. Teachers College Press.

4 Inclusive assessment

As educators, we have all found ourselves, at some point in time, wondering how to best engage a particular student or a group of students. Maybe one of these scenarios resonates with you:

Box 4.1

A new student, Ly, arrives in your classroom with limited English proficiency and they, initially, choose not to speak. There are no other students in the classroom who speak the same language. Ly's silence causes concern from their teachers as they do not know how to communicate with Ly.

Tommy finds social interactions difficult and, as a result, he struggles with collaborative tasks. He likes being able to have routines and clear and concise information. He can easily become overwhelmed particularly with new topics or tasks.

While Zain is in Year 7, he is currently working through the Year 4 mathematics curriculum. He is a refugee and has had many years of interrupted schooling as he had limited access to formal education. It is difficult for him to be so far behind the other students academically, which results in him choosing not to attend school most days.

Emily is a high-ability student with a passion for literature and writing. While academically she is very strong, her teacher notices that she seems to disengage in classroom activities.

How to best engage our students continues to be a common topic discussed in the staffroom. We share with our colleagues strategies that have worked in the past in similar situations to differentiate our teaching and provide appropriate learning conditions. For example, how we might provide information in a range of different ways and modalities. For Ly and Tommy, having visual cues, gestures and concise written instructions helps by providing clear

DOI: 10.4324/9781032657219-4

communication. When considering how to accommodate different ways of learning, we might provide different ways for students to demonstrate their understanding of a topic or skill by giving them different options to choose from. This would allow Emily to choose a mode of learning that might challenge her, while Zain could choose something he felt would enable him to successfully demonstrate what he has learned (as we should with all learners).

However, while most teachers are aware of the need to differentiate how they teach and to provide accommodations for how students learn, there is often less attention given to differentiating how we assess students. Most of the hesitation is grounded in the idea that assessment needs to be objective as this makes it more valid and reliable. As a result, many believe that assessments must ensure that every learner has the same prompts, questions and conditions—ultimately a one-size-fits-all approach. However, the good news is that we *can* have assessment tasks that are both inclusive *and* valid and reliable (see Chapter 1 to refresh your understanding of these terms). The idea that assessments need to be the same for everyone has been driven by the use of standardised testing. Standardised tests are designed to be used across a large cohort of students and produce a large data set. It is important to note that standardised tests are not necessarily more valid and reliable than other educational assessments[1] and to be valid they also need to be fit for purpose.[2] As mentioned in Chapter 1, unfortunately, there is no such thing as a perfect assessment. When designing or evaluating an assessment, it is about making decisions about the purpose of the assessment task (see Box 3.3 in Chapter 3). If the assessment task is intended to be used to compare groups of students across classes, schools or jurisdictions, reliability and **practicality** may be high on the priority list. However, if you are designing or using an assessment for your classroom, you might focus primarily on ensuring that the assessment is fit for purpose and will provide meaningful and relevant opportunities for your diverse group of students to demonstrate their learning.

To explore ways in which assessment can be both inclusive and engaging, this chapter has two main aims. The first is to examine how educators can create inclusive assessments that are valid and reliable yet allow students to demonstrate their learning in a diverse classroom. We will draw upon the Universal Design for Learning principles, which has been used to support differentiation in teaching and learning, but with a focus on assessment. Secondly, this chapter will explore how we can use assessment to engage our students by exploring the different types of student engagement, namely behavioural, cognitive, emotional/affective and agentic and how we might harness assessment to encourage student engagement in our classrooms.

Creating inclusive assessments

Before we begin unpacking how the principles of the Universal Design for Learning (UDL) guidelines[3] can be applied to designing and choosing appropriate assessments, it is important to understand what we mean by 'inclusive.'

While **inclusive education** is often used, more specifically, to describe the inclusion of students with special education needs (SEN),[4] the notion of *inclusion* in education is much broader in scope and often used in a social justice approach to education. Within a social justice frame, there is a focus on the inclusion of students regardless of their *individual* differences. These individual differences can be based on ability, race, culture, language background and/or proficiency, disability, gender, sexuality and socioeconomic status. This approach pushes back against deficit views in education that view students with individual differences for what they lack instead of what they contribute.[5]

The goal of inclusive education is to provide **equitable opportunities** for all students to succeed academically, socially and emotionally. It is also important to note the difference between equity and equality in education and how this relates to inclusive education. Inclusive education is not about providing everyone with equal opportunities or the same opportunities as some students will be advantaged or disadvantaged in this situation. Instead, it is about acknowledging the systemic barriers and disparities that exist and result in some students having more access to educational opportunities while others require more support. This requires teachers to differentiate how they respond and cater for the needs of their students.[6]

The UDL guidelines provide educators with suggestions that ensure all students have access to and can fully participate in learning opportunities. The guidelines are grounded in cognitive neuroscience research and provide suggestions on how educators can design learning environments that draw upon what we know about the brain and support all learners.[7] UDL acknowledges that while an 'average brain' does not exist and there are no two brains that are alike, the human brain has incredible **plasticity**. Neural connections are made stronger and faster when we learn but can weaken if not used. In other words, learning must be viewed as growth over time. This is why a developmental approach to assessment is so important. As educators, if we recognise that the brain has the ability to constantly grow and change, we need to track this growth and development. Luckily, this is the precise aim of competency-based assessment as we recognise that competencies, which are the interconnectedness of knowledge, skills, attitudes, values and behaviours, can be explicitly taught and tracked over time.

It is beyond the scope of this book to explore the guidelines in detail so we encourage you to explore the range of UDL online resources for a more in-depth understanding.[8] In most cases, UDL is applied to how teachers teach and how students learn, we will explore how UDL principles can be applied to assessment.

There are three UDL key principles:

- Provide multiple means of representation.
- Provide multiple means of action and expression.
- Provide multiple means of engagement.

So how do we apply the UDL principles to assessment more generally and competency-based assessment more specifically?

Multiple means of representation

In relation to how the brain works and how we learn, the first principle focuses on providing multiple means of representation which highlights that learning is influenced by how information is processed and retained. The principle focuses on ensuring that learners are provided a range of ways to experience and process information. Many of the UDL suggestions focus on modality, or the format in which information is presented. For example, it is encouraged that educators provide a range of alternative modes to present information (visual, auditory, written) and are flexible in knowing and then addressing the unique needs of their students. This is not to suggest that students' achievement is tied to a particular learning 'style' (e.g., visual, auditory and kinaesthetic)[9] but that alternatives and/or accommodations may be required for some students to provide additional support and that presenting information in multiple modes *reinforces* learning. For example, for language learners (e.g., those with limited language proficiency in the medium of instruction) and learners from neurodiverse backgrounds, key language and ideas can be reinforced further when presented both orally and with corresponding visuals.

In our experience with assessment, the ways in which an assessment task's instructions and key information are presented to students is important but often not always given the consideration that is required. We have incorporated our observations surrounding the design and implementation of assessment tasks to provide suggestions on how to better apply UDL.

Information overload. The first step in designing assessment instructions is to determine what is essential information and what is not. Reducing **extraneous** details helps in supporting and regulating cognitive processing as students only have to focus on the key information rather than being distracted by a range of details which they must then determine what to prioritise.[10] In addition, the process of carefully reviewing and simplifying the instructions can provide more clarity for you, as the educator, as you allow for additional time to consider what exactly you are teaching and assessing, what students are being asked to do and what they need to know at different points in time. For large assessment tasks that might consist of several steps, it is important to break down the task into manageable steps and parts so that students are not overwhelmed by the enormity and/or complexity of the task. A brief overview can be provided in a visual (e.g., diagram or table) but decisions will need to be made about what information should be presented and when, with a focus on only providing the information that is relevant at that point in time.

Written/verbal presentation of information. In most assessment tasks, there are written instructions that are accompanied by verbal explanations. Firstly, if written and verbal instructions are to be used, ensure ample time for preparation to consider what information will be presented to students. While written explanations are often more thought-out, verbal instructions

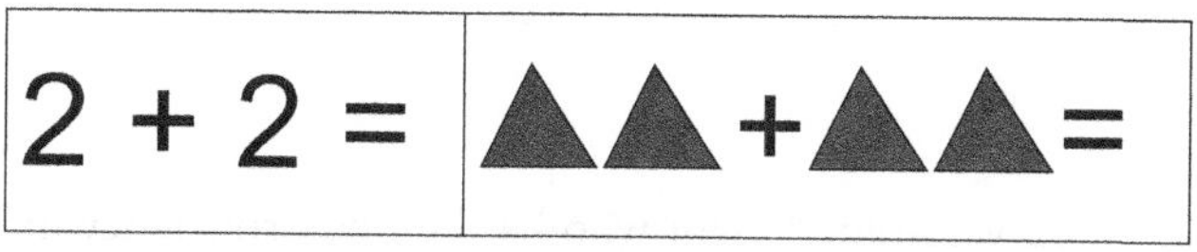

$$2 + 2 = \quad \blacktriangle\blacktriangle + \blacktriangle\blacktriangle =$$

Figure 4.1 Presenting the same information in different ways.

can become confusing for students and sometimes contradictory to written instructions. Additionally, you will have students who struggle to understand lengthy verbal instructions (e.g., students with limited language proficiency or students with neurodevelopmental disorders). Therefore, ensure that verbal instructions are planned and reflect the needs of your students. Regardless of students' individual needs, being concise and clear is appreciated by all. The use of generative AI can be a helpful tool in minimising jargon and ensuring that instructions are concise.

Secondly, consider the use of visuals (e.g., diagrams, tables, pictures) to accompany both written instructions and the assessment content. Visual cues can be provided to help scaffold and support students' recognition of key concepts and ideas by recognising that information can be presented (and, therefore, understood and reinforced) in multiple ways. A very simple example is to consider multiple ways to present the same information, as in Figure 4.1. (see Figure 4.1).

Providing worked examples. We strongly believe that for students to fully understand how to approach an assessment task, they need to understand what the performance or the completion of the task looks like. While the assessment task should reflect previous learning tasks/topics and concepts, teachers need to ensure that students know how best to complete or approach the task. Firstly, we suggest using **worked examples**, or a step-by-step demonstrations of how to solve a problem or perform a task, which walk through the steps and thinking required to address a particular task and is an approach that has an influence on student learning.[11] In addition, to providing worked examples, students need to understand what criterion is being used to assess their performance and how. In particular, they need to understand the differences between what a performance at a novice or beginning level looks like in comparison with one that is more advanced. This is important because this helps students understand that learning occurs as part of a continuum. The one-size-fits-all approach suggests that to successfully demonstrate your learning, you need to get the "A" but unfortunately, for some, the A is neither accessible nor possible at that particular point in time. Students can feel quite defeated and motivation and engagement with the task may wane. However, when performance is seen as part of a continuum where students can track their progress, we push against the notion that there is a standard for all and focus on the belief that students can and do develop over time when engaged in learning processes. The following scenario provides an example of how students and teachers might view and support this approach.

Box 4.2

Marcella is a 12-year-old student who has limited proficiency in English and recently began school in an English-speaking country. Marcella feels frustrated due to her limited language proficiency which creates barriers in being able to demonstrate her understanding and ideas effectively. The class has been asked to complete a written assessment task and she is worried that she will fail the task because when compared with her peers, her written language ability is limited. However, despite her concerns, the teacher has designed a developmental rubric, which provides a continuum of performance (see Chapter 5 for more about developmental rubrics), that clearly explains what a novice-level written response looks like compared to a more advanced one. Marcella understands that the goal is not perfection but improvement over time. Like the other students in the classroom, Marcella identifies where she currently sits within the continuum and then identifies the next progression level up. She then works with her teacher to identify learning goals to help her meet her target progression point on the rubric. She uses this continuum to help her understand where she is in her learning and where she needs to go, while her teacher identifies what targeted instruction is required to help her meet her goals.

Multiple means of action and expression

While the first UDL principle focuses on how teachers can present information in different ways to support and enhance student understanding and learning, the second principle is about giving students options and choices in how they go about their learning (e.g., process of learning) and how they present and communicate their understanding (e.g., product of learning). As argued in this book, we view assessment as more than the product of learning but also the process, which aligns well with this second principle. The following are some assessment considerations of how students might be provided with options and choices in the assessment process (see also Chapter 6).

Providing flexibility and access. The guidelines for UDL suggest that students should be provided learning resources that allow them to actively navigate and interact without being disadvantaged. For example, considerations need to be made if a student has a movement impairment (e.g., including their ability to type) or other barriers that may limit their ability to interact with learning materials or resources. The use of online assessments is increasingly being used in classrooms as they are on-demand and can easily be used to compare students across a range of cohorts, schools and districts/states/territories. However, like any assessment, there needs to be thoughtful consideration of the barriers that might influence a student's ability to demonstrate their understanding and the opportunities that such an assessment might afford learners. For example, assistive technologies can support students with learning barriers and can also be used to support students with limited language proficiency (e.g., providing translation tools). Another consideration is the time constraints for assessment tasks. Timed tests are another convention of the one-size-fits-all argument that intimates that for a test to be fair and reliable, everyone needs to be evaluated based on the same conditions. We agree that for a test to be as reliable as possible, we should attempt to ensure consistency within the assessment itself and process, however, ***not at the cost of jeopardising a student's ability to demonstrate their understanding***. Providing time limits may seemingly ensure that there are consistent conditions for all students so that they might be judged equally but it will ultimately impact the validity of the results. If an assessment is not valid, efforts to ensure that it is reliable are meaningless. Ultimately, when applying UDL to assessment practice, educators need to ensure that assessments are valid for all their students. In order to achieve this, they will need to ensure that there are no barriers, or barriers are minimised, to demonstrating their understanding and that they are provided with a range of assistive technologies to provide them with access. This is an example of equitable practice as educators understand that to even the playing field, some students will need additional support and flexibility to reduce existing barriers.

Goal setting, support and monitoring during the assessment process. UDL guidelines encourage teachers to create environments in which both teachers and students can set goals and strategise how student learning might progress. However, to help support students in this process, as discussed in the next point, teachers need to have a clear understanding of what and how to observe student performance (their demonstration of knowledge, skills, attitudes, values and/or behaviours) and how to help them progress on a learning continuum. This is why having developmental rubrics or frameworks can help in naming and describing what students can do at a particular level – from novice to expert (see Chapter 5). We provide an excerpt from our communication framework that we piloted in 2023, as shown in Figure 4.2. In this framework, the sub-capability is delivering communication (for communication there are three different sub-capabilities: delivering communication, receiving communication and designing communication). Delivering communication is further broken up into indicative behaviours, or indicators, with quality criteria describing what development looks like.

Once the framework/developmental rubric is introduced to students, teachers need to work alongside them to identify where they are on the learning continuum so they can set goals and identify the knowledge, skills and strategies needed to progress to the next level. Unfortunately, this is often where teachers struggle. If the levels of performance are not clear and/or understood by teachers,[12] it will be difficult for them to identify what to observe regarding student performance and then scaffold students appropriately with

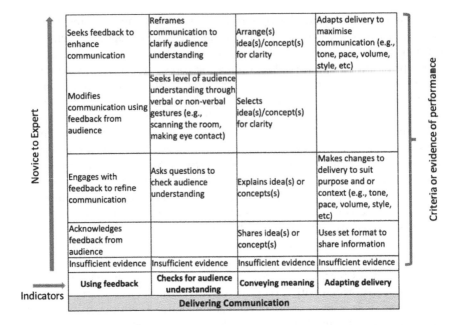

Figure 4.2 An excerpt from a communication framework (Version 2, 2023).

relevant explicit teaching and guidance. Teachers first need to have clear ways to track student development and then identify frequent points in time, or checkpoints, in which they can interpret and apply assessment data to their instructional design. Assessment data do not just have to be a 'product' or an end-of-unit/term/semester assessment task but the observation and monitoring of the assessment process, which can include the observation of students' use of strategies, their attitudes and their performance on the relevant task more specifically. Once teachers know where students are at, where they are going and how to scaffold them in the process, they can create environments that encourage students to actively play a role in the assessment process.

Multiple means of engagement

While the next section will go into more depth about the role of engagement in assessment, this section will discuss how the third UDL principle, which acknowledges that learners differ in their engagement and motivation in learning, applies to assessment. This section will identify some of the ways in which teachers might design and implement assessment practices and processes that maximise opportunities for student engagement.

Connections and meaning beyond the school classroom. One of the reasons why we argue that competency-based assessment is important for students' futures is because the development of competencies can support the navigation and success of future studies, employment and everyday life. The development of competencies, for example, critical thinking, will not only support a student as they complete a standardised assessment task but is required for success beyond the school classroom. Therefore, when assessing competencies, it needs to be very clear why students are learning these competencies and how students' development might be applied to situations in and beyond the classroom.

For both teachers and students to value the development of competencies, their value and relevance for both academic study and future life need to be extremely clear.

Creating safe and productive spaces. In order to create a safe and productive place for students to learn, we often try to ensure that the classroom environment is supportive. In relation to assessment, we need to ensure that we create a safe space to *fail* and make *mistakes*. We find it confusing that while we dislike calling out and discussing failure explicitly, as it seems so negative and causes anxiety among young people, we are happy to argue the importance of resilience. A core aspect of resilience is that when you face challenges, or you experience failure, you can persist, cope and eventually manage the situation. A number of school-based interventions have attempted to address anxiety and depression among school-aged children and adolescents,[13] which speaks to a heightened awareness that many young people struggle with mental health. However, we argue that supportive classroom environments allow students opportunities to make mistakes and learn from them, and this can support rather than hinder their mental health. Resilience is about learning how to a cope and manage challenges and so when we think about assessment, we first need to view mistakes and failure as an opportunity to grow and develop. A developmental approach to assessment, rather than an end-of-unit/term/ semester test, allows for students to focus on where they are at and how to progress rather than always comparing them to a standard (e.g., mastery of key concepts and ideas) and the extent to which they failed to meet this standard. Additionally, as argued in the previous section, when designing and choosing assessment tasks, we need to identify and minimise barriers (what barriers exist that will make it difficult for students to fully demonstrate their knowledge and understanding) and then be flexible in making accommodations. This will then create an environment where assessment is an opportunity for both teachers and students to identify where students are at in their learning and where to next instead of creating environments where only some seemingly succeed.

Providing students with agency in how (and what) to demonstrate. In aligning with a developmental approach to assessment and competency-based assessment more specifically, students, as argued above, need to be part of planning and monitoring of their learning. However, if we provide opportunities for students to plan for and monitor their learning, then we also need to provide opportunities for them to gain a sense of **agency** in how they demonstrate their learning. Student agency refers to the capacity of students to make choices, set goals and take responsibility for their education, which in turn, fosters a sense of ownership and empowerment in the learning process. The UDL guidelines suggest that students should be given an option to use a choice of modalities to express their understanding and how they are progressing in their learning. This is because no particular mode of expression equally suits all learners. However, this does not mean that teachers limit the development and assessment of modes of expression that prove difficult for students. For example, a student with dyslexia may be able to present their ideas more easily (and validly) in a short presentation than they would be able to do in a written report. If the aim of the assessment is primarily to assess their ability to identify and present information on a topic rather than specifically on the mode of presentation – e.g., written, oral or multimodal – then students should be given opportunities to choose how they express their knowledge and ideas. As mentioned before, just because students struggle to express their knowledge in a particular mode does not mean that we should never assess this, but clarity needs to be provided in what is being assessed and if the mode of presentation is not the focus of the assessment, then the assessment can still be a valid measure without choosing one form of expression over another. It is important to acknowledge that students have preferences in how they express and communicate their learning. Therefore, teachers need to ensure that there are options for students when the purpose of the assessment does not intend to measure the mode of expression (e.g., written expression). Additionally, teachers need to assess frequently and provide variety in how students express and communicate their knowledge rather than favouring a particular mode. It is common for some teachers to favour a mode (e.g., written or oral) based on how they like to express and communicate and/or how they prefer to assess work. In addition to providing alternative and varied modalities for expression, it is important to allow students to be an active part of the assessment process. There is a relationship between students' sense of ownership of their learning process, or agency, and their engagement. As a result, when students feel like they have a choice, or agency, in what and how they are assessed, there is the potential for increased motivation and engagement levels (see Chapter 6). In addition to providing students with an opportunity to make decisions during the assessment process, UDL guidelines also suggest that to support student agency, teachers need to provide them with access to a range of resources so they can choose which of these might best support them in the process. This might include a range of different technological tools that support text-to-speech, grammar and word choice checks and so on.

Student engagement: Assessment for Engagement (AfE)

As educators, we want to ensure that students are actively involved in the process of learning and so we must spend time planning how we might gain students' interest and curiosity about a topic or skill. We now build upon the discussion about UDL's multiple means of engagement to consider whether engagement could be considered a *purpose* of assessment (see Chapter 1).

Before we discuss the relationship between engagement and assessment regarding the purposes of assessment, we first need to consider the different dimensions of engagement. This is important because we often think of engagement in light of what we can easily observe. The child sleeping on his desk might indicate he is not very engaged, while the reality is that he may have the desire, but other factors are influencing his ability to engage. This type of engagement is called **behavioural engagement**. This engagement is often limited to what we can observe, such as their participation and involvement in tasks and activities whether independent, collaborative and/or whole class. As educators, we recognise students who are are actively participating in discussions and/or asking and answering questions in class. This type of engagement is behavioural but often what is thought of first when we consider whether or not students are *engaged*.

Cognitive engagement, on the other hand, is not always observed in behaviours but is often identified in students' learning processes and products. For example, we might view this type of engagement in the mental effort that is put forth in students' learning tasks. While this is not to be confused with a student's ability as students may differ in their ability, cognitive engagement is more about students' effort and focus on a task and their ability to regulate their learning. Competency-based assessment aligns well with the notion of cognitive engagement as teachers can encourage cognitive engagement by designing learning (or process-based assessment) tasks that encourage students to use and demonstrate competencies such as problem-solving and critical thinking to engage with the subject matter. The use of such competencies requires students to employ these competencies as cognitive strategies to complete their tasks.

While student engagement can be understood in relation to students' behaviours and cognitive effort and focus, **emotional or affective engagement** refers to students' emotional connections to their learning. This type of engagement is important because learning and/or assessment can easily be influenced by one's emotions and ultimately, we want students to be interested and enjoy what they are learning and being assessed on. If students value and enjoy what they are learning (and learning has been targeted at their level or achievable above their level), they will likely be more motivated to progress their learning due to their positive attitudes towards the topic or subject. However, teachers need to address any existing emotional barriers to learning (e.g., mathematics anxiety) when attempting to make learning of interest or more meaningful to students.

Finally, another aspect of engagement has recently received more attention as it attempts to better capture the role of students in the process of learning. Behavioural, cognitive and emotional engagement are often shaped by the conditions of the learning environment (e.g., teachers' design of tasks and their ability to create an engaging classroom environment); **agentic engagement**, on the other hand, is about how students' proactively influence the classroom environment.[14]

Now that we understand the different dimensions of engagement, how does this relate to assessment? In Chapter 1, we identified different purposes of assessment which were categorised in the following ways:

- Assessment of learning (AoL) is often associated with summative assessment tasks at the end of a unit/term/semester and focuses on the achievement or mastery of key terms and ideas.
- Assessment for learning (AfL) is often associated with formative assessments throughout a unit/term/semester and focuses on the learning process.
- Assessment as learning (AaL) involves engaging students in self and peer assessment.
- Diagnostic assessments determine what students already know about a topic, skill or behaviour.

We suggest that Assessment for Engagement (AfE) is another purpose of assessment that educators need to understand and embed in their instructional design with a focus on considering how they are positioning student learning and engagement within the assessment process. We suggest that AfE extends upon the purpose of AaL and encapsulates the following:

- Assessment for Learning (AfE) involves engaging students in the process of assessment (including peer and self-assessment) as well as actively monitoring their engagement (behavioural, cognitive, emotional and agentic) and approaches and strategies to learning, which we attempt to visualise in Figure 4.3.

In an attempt to further understand the relationship between engagement, learning and assessment, we conclude this section with three key insights into the use of competency-based assessment in schools.

Firstly, teachers, students and parents *care* about assessment and as a result, there is an opportunity to utilise assessment to engage students (and parents/carers). We have come to understand that what is documented and/or tracked in assessment is what is often deemed important by key stakeholders, such as teachers, students and parents/carers. This is because it is not possible to assess, track and report all aspects of student learning, so decisions must be made on what should be assessed. However, in making these decisions, aspects of learning are valued and/or prioritised over other aspects. We argue that as educators, we should take advantage of the status of assessment. A key reason for wanting to assess competencies is that when they are not assessed (and/or documented) nor communicated as learning to students to parents, they are not prioritised by teachers, students or parents/carers. If competencies are not assessed, teachers will often not prioritise them in their planning or embed them meaningfully in their instructional design. Likewise, students and parents/carers will prioritise learning that is made visible and contributes to how the school views achievement.

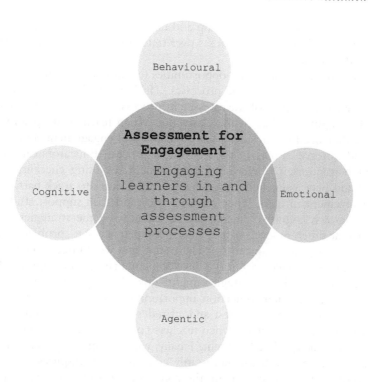

Figure 4.3 Assessment for Engagement: Harnessing the dimensions of engagement to better engage students in the assessment process.

Secondly, if we want to galvanise the relationship between student engagement, learning and assessment, we must ensure that students are part of the assessment process (see more on this in Chapter 6). If educators are willing to shift towards a more developmental approach to assessment and want to meaningfully track student progress, then we need students to be part of this process. While traditionally assessment has often been viewed as teacher-driven and controlled (see Chapter 1, Figure 1.1) in which assessment is done to students by teachers, we argue that assessment is an integral part of the teaching and learning process and while teachers do have a role in planning for learning, students still need to view assessment as part of their learning process. Therefore, students need to be active participants and not just objects of assessment. We would argue that a key purpose of competency-based assessment is engagement. We want to ensure that students view competency-based learning as part of a learning continuum that starts when they are young and continues into adulthood. They need to see the development of competencies, for example, communication, as something that they continue to develop and refine in different contexts (e.g., school, extra-curricular activities, work settings) and over time. We need students to understand that they do not 'master' a competency in Year 7 and then there is no longer the need to progress but rather that they continue to develop and test their understanding and ability to demonstrate in different contexts over time, a process that is intentionally scaffolded by educators.

As educators, we can create opportunities for monitoring student engagement in assessment tasks and processes. Having established that students should be a central part of the assessment process, it is important to identify what this might look like in the classroom. When teachers are planning for learning they need to consider what dimensions of engagement they want to track and observe as part of the assessment process. Educators can observe student behaviours, or behavioural engagement, by using checklists (utilising self and peer assessment) or using anecdotal notes to track participation and involvement in tasks. They can also track and then support students to track their own cognitive engagement by identifying the strategies that are linked to the different levels of a particular competence (e.g., problem-solving, critical thinking, communication). These strategies would need to be embedded and clearly defined within the developmental rubric and supported with examples of what these strategies might look like in practice. In addition, self-assessment, frequent reflection opportunities and teacher check-ins can be used to track student interest and attitudes toward the assessment which can then be used as feedback when teachers consider what and how they will teach (or re-teach) related content. Finally, while agentic engagement is not something that teachers can necessarily control as this requires students to make choices, teachers can create the conditions to support this. Chapter 6 will explore how teachers might create such environments that allow students to be more agentic in the assessment process.

Validity and one-size-fits-all

This section briefly explores the research surrounding the adoption of a one-size-fits-all approach to assessment. As mentioned earlier, this one-size-fits-all approach stems from the notion that if we have a standard measurement of assessment, then we can ensure that the assessment is valid and fair. Assessment, particularly standardised assessment, has often been driven by **psychometric testing**. This approach is grounded in a **positivist**, assessment paradigm and views assessment as something that can be diagnosed, compared and rated in a standardised and consistent way.[15] However, the very validity of a standardised test comes into question if it does not consider its potential bias regarding the diversity of its test takers.[16] Therefore, it is not only how assessments are designed that may advantage particular groups and disadvantage others, but how the assessment results are then interpreted to advantage some over others.

While interpreting assessment results can provide meaningful accommodations in teaching, learning and assessment, sometimes these results are used to further solidify differences and disadvantage as proactive and equitable teaching and learning strategies are never applied. Standardised testing aims to compare students regardless of their differences and/or needs and, therefore, it is not used to celebrate and track the progress over time. Data are continually scrutinised regarding the achievement gaps between student populations in standardised tests, such as Indigenous and non-Indigenous students;[17] however, there is less focus on discussing how we monitor and track the *progress of achievement over time* to address these achievement gaps. We argue that we will never bridge achievement gaps if we continue to prioritise a standardised view of assessment. While standardised assessment does have a role in education, schools and teachers need to embrace a developmental approach to assessment if they want to ensure that assessment is inclusive and actively engages students in the learning process.

Chapter summary and reflection

As educators, we understand that an inclusive approach to teaching and learning is important for fostering an educational environment that values diversity and supports all students. However, this also extends to assessment practices, where inclusivity understands and caters for differences and readily addresses barriers that might limit some students' ability to demonstrate their understanding and ability. Integrating the principles of Universal Design for Learning (UDL) and prioritising student engagement in the design of assessment products and the scaffolding of assessment practices further enhances an inclusive approach to education. In considering how assessment can not only engage students but provide opportunities for inclusion, reflect on the following:

1 Consider your current assessment practices: What <u>types</u> of assessments do you use and for what <u>purpose</u>? <u>How often do</u> you assess your students? What do you assess (do you assess everything)? How do you go about collecting and interpreting assessment data? Now consider these questions again in light of teh diversity of students in your classroom. First identify the barriers that might restrict some students from fully engaging in the assessment process (e.g., physical, cognitive). How might you accommodate student needs in a way that allows them to demonstrate their knowledge and understanding without being limited by these barriers? What specific assessment strategies might you use to cater for diverse learners in your classroom?

2 Reflect on a current assessment task or activity. Use the following steps to reflect on the task:

   a Are the instructions clear, concise and explicit? Are there examples, models or visuals to help clarify expectations?

   b Are there any barriers that might prevent students from actively engaging in the assessment process? Does it require typing or any other physical movements? Are there any potential distractions (e.g., noise, lighting)?

   c Are there multiple means of expression or action? If the mode of expression is not assessed, are students given choices and options in how they will present their understanding?

   d Is there opportunity for flexibility to support students (e.g., timing, layout)?

   e Can technology be used to allow for better access (e.g., size of font, support for vocabulary and/or grammar)?

3 In considering future practice, how might you use assessment to engage students in the process of learning (particularly tracking their own progress). How might you incorporate this into your instructional design?

Notes

1 Wiliam, D. (2001). Reliability, validity, and all that jazz. *Education 3–13, 29*(3), 17–21.
2 Baird, J.-A., Andrich, D., Hopfenbeck, T.N., & Stobart, G. (2017). Assessment and learning: Fields apart? *Assessment in Education: Principles, Policy & Practice, 24*(3), 317–350. https://doi.org/10.1080/0969594X.2017.1319337.
3 CAST (2011). *Universal design for learning guidelines version 2.0*. Wakefield, MA: Author.
4 Ewing, D.L., Monsen, J.J., & Kielblock, S. (2018). Teachers' attitudes towards inclusive education: A critical review of published questionnaires. *Educational Psychology in Practice, 34*(2), 150–165.
5 Amina, F., Barnes, M., & Saito, E. (2023). Exploring teachers' understanding of and responses to the school belonging experiences of students from refugee backgrounds. *Teaching Education*. https://doi.org/10.1080/10476210.2023.2291387.
6 Cardona-Escobar, D., Pruyn, M., & Barnes, M. (2021). Colombian national bilingual plan: A vehicle for equity or an instrument for accountability? *Journal of Multilingual and Multicultural Development*, 1–14.
7 CAST. (2018). *UDL and the learning brain*. Wakefield, MA: Author. Retrieved from http://www.cast.org/products-services/resources/2018/udl-learning-brain-neuroscience.
8 CAST. (2024). *Tips and free resources*. Retrieved on 9 January, 2024: https://www.cast.org/resources/tips-free.
9 An, D., & Carr, M. (2017). Learning styles theory fails to explain learning and achievement: Recommendations for alternative approaches. *Personality and Individual Differences, 116*, 410–416.
10 Klepsch, M., & Seufert, T. (2020). Understanding instructional design effects by differentiated measurement of intrinsic, extraneous, and germane cognitive load. *Instructional Science, 48*(1), 45–77.
11 Barbieri, C.A., Miller-Cotto, D., Clerjuste, S.N., & Chawla, K. (2023). A meta-analysis of the worked examples effect on mathematics performance. *Educational Psychology Review, 35*(1), 11.
12 Brown, T.D., Barnes, M., & Finefter-Rosenbluh, I. (2024). Teacher perspectives and experiences of assessment literacy in victorian junior secondary schools. *Australian Journal of Education, 68*(1), 5–22. https://doi.org/10.1177/00049441231214022.
13 Zhang, Q., Wang, J., & Neitzel, A. (2023). School-based mental health interventions targeting depression or anxiety: A meta-analysis of rigorous randomized controlled trials for school-aged children and adolescents. *Journal of Youth and Adolescence, 52*, 195–217. https://doi.org/10.1007/s10964-022-01684-4.
14 Patall, E.A., Pituch, K.A., Steingut, R.R., Vasquez, A.C., Yates, N., & Kennedy, A.A. (2019). Agency and high school science students' motivation, engagement,

and classroom support experiences. *Journal of Applied Developmental Psychology*, *62*, 77–92.

15 Levy-Feldman, I., & Libman, Z. (2022). One size doesn't fit all educational assessment in a multicultural and intercultural world. *Intercultural Education*, *33*(4), 380–390.

16 Van der Vijver, A.J.R., & Rothmann, S. (2004). Assessment in multicultural groups: The South African case. *SA Journal of Industrial Psychology*, *30*(4), 1–7.

17 Cumming, J., Goldstein, H., & Hand, K. (2020). Enhanced use of educational accountability data to monitor educational progress of Australian students with a focus on Indigenous students. *Educational Assessment, Evaluation and Accountability*, *32*, 29–51.

5 Making sense of assessment data and evidence

Take a moment to think about the last television series or movie you watched that involved a court case. There is often high drama associated with witnesses, admissible evidence and the jury being instructed to 'disregard' any inadmissible evidence. The deliberations, brief or lengthy, often highlight the ways juries work with the evidence to reach a verdict. What does this have to do with teaching and learning? Surprisingly, quite a bit. The verdict in educational contexts is about what students know or can do, rather than guilt or innocence. For students, the outcome of the verdict may be high stakes, such as entry to a special program or course. Or, the outcome may impact the quality and degree of learning; for example, being given tasks that are too easy or hard. Either way, the judgements about student learning will have a direct impact on the student so we too should consider the quality, or admissibility, of our evidence.

Teachers, schools and school systems collect a plethora of data on a regular basis. The data may be:

- student achievement scores on a national or international assessment program such as NAPLAN or PISA,
- student attendance data,
- parent/caregiver/guardian opinion surveys.

For classroom teachers, the data collected will likely be used to make a judgement about student learning. This judgement may be used to inform planning, to ascertain how much has been learnt or to provide feedback to the learner.

Data can take many forms, including text, observations, numbers, percentages, graphs, symbols or figures. Data on its own has no meaning. Consider the following dataset:

Data: 6, 7, 9, 9, 10, 5

In this format, the data are just a set of numbers. There is no context and as such they are meaningless. They could be the results of a test but we do not know if it was out of 10/20/50 or the construct being assessed. They could be the number of days absent from school, or they could be shoe sizes! Data becomes

DOI: 10.4324/9781032657219-5

evidence when we use it as 'evidence for or of something.' In other words, we are using it to support an argument, opinion, viewpoint or hypothesis.

Evidence of student learning

Evidence must be directly observable. Evidence is what students 'do, say, make and write' and can be recorded in some way need to insert a reference here. Reference is Griffin, P. (2018). Assessment as the search for evidence of learning. In P. Griffin (Ed.), *Assessment for teaching* (2nd ed., pp. 14-25) Cambridge University Press. https://doi.org/10.1017/9781108116053.008. Teachers can't see what a student 'thinks,' as they can't see what is going on in the brain. However, they can see how students respond, which is indicative of students' progress and learning needs.

Think of all the different ways teachers and schools use assessment. Assessments can be used:

- to identify what students are ready to learn,
- as the basis for reporting to parents,
- to determine access to differentiated provisions (for example, accelerated pathways, learning support),
- to measure the impact of teaching,
- to make adjustments to learning (formative),
- to set goals for and with students,
- to evaluate programs,
- for admission to tertiary courses.

The list goes on. Some of these are high stakes, others less so. But the one thing they all have in common is that the evidence is based on the data collected in the first instance. Reflect on the courtroom drama and inadmissible evidence. What is the equivalent in education? How often do we consider the quality of evidence and how often do we rule assessment evidence as inadmissible? The most obvious example is when a student is caught cheating. If it is not their own work, then it cannot be used as evidence of their learning. But there are other reasons or circumstances that would render evidence from an assessment 'inadmissible.'

What is quality evidence?

We introduced the idea of quality evidence in Chapter 2 as an important consideration in assessment design. This is because noise, or measurement errors, are factors that contribute to the collection of inaccurate data (which should be ruled inadmissible). There are many sources of 'noise' and there are strategies that can be put in place to reduce noise. One example of noise might be the quality of instructions administered to the students. There are many funny examples on the internet that illustrate how test item wording can be ambiguous and confusing. Other sources of noise include the student (were they sick on the day of the assessment?), the context (was it administered on a Friday afternoon?), the teacher (were there distractions?) and the task. Box 5.1 provides a reminder of the questions that can be used to determine quality evidence.

Box 5.1   Questions to review for quality evidence

Is the evidence...
  Valid?

- Has the learning outcome been considered?
- Is the task consistent with the purpose of the assessment?
- Is it at an appropriate level?

Sufficient?

- Is there sufficient evidence to enable an accurate level of competency? (i.e., avoids the shopping list approach)
- Is there a balance of direct and indirect evidence?

Authentic?

- Is this the students' own work?

Current?

- The work is of the current student at the current time

Consistent?

- The evidence has been collected over time and in different contexts to ensure there is a consistent demonstration of competencies in the learning outcomes

---

How do we record evidence?

How do teachers organise their assessment data, whether they be formative, diagnostic or summative data? Even with the prevalence of spreadsheets and other online tools for recording results, some teachers still prefer to keep a record in mark books where ticks indicate correct responses and the crosses indicate incorrect responses, as shown in Figure 5.1. This works for tests or situations where there is a correct/incorrect or yes/no response (known as dichotomous data). A percentage is typically calculated based on the raw score and in some cases, a grade is assigned based on this.

Student	1	2	3	4	5	6	7	8	9	10	11	12	13	14	15	16	17	Raw score
Adam Zapel	✓	✓	✓	✗	✓	✓	✓	✗	✗	✓	✗	✓	✓	✓	✓	✓	✓	13
Al Dente	✓	✓	✓	✗	✓	✗	✓	✓	✗	✗	✓	✓	✓	✓	✓	✓	✓	13
Alf A. Romeo	✓	✓	✓	✗	✗	✓	✗	✗	✓	✗	✓	✓	✗	✓	✗	✓	✗	9
Ali Gaither	✓	✗	✓	✗	✓	✗	✗	✗	✓	✗	✗	✗	✗	✓	✗	✗	✗	5
B.A. Ware	✓	✓	✓	✓	✓	✓	✗	✓	✓	✗	✗	✓	✗	✗	✗	✓	✗	9
Barb Dwyer	✗	✓	✓	✗	✓	✗	✓	✓	✓	✗	✗	✓	✗	✗	✓	✓	✗	9
Cara Van	✓	✓	✓	✗	✓	✓	✓	✓	✗	✗	✗	✓	✗	✓	✓	✓	✓	12
Carrie Oakey	✓	✓	✓	✗	✓	✗	✓	✗	✗	✗	✗	✗	✗	✗	✗	✗	✗	5
Doris Schutt	✓	✓	✓	✓	✓	✓	✓	✓	✓	✗	✗	✓	✗	✓	✓	✓	✓	14
Earl E. Bird	✗	✓	✗	✗	✓	✗	✗	✓	✗	✗	✗	✗	✗	✓	✗	✗	✗	4
Gene Poole	✓	✓	✓	✓	✓	✓	✓	✗	✓	✓	✓	✓	✓	✓	✓	✓	✓	16
Heidi Clare	✓	✓	✓	✓	✗	✓	✓	✓	✓	✓	✓	✓	✓	✓	✓	✓	✓	16
Hugh Morris	✓	✓	✓	✓	✓	✓	✓	✗	✓	✗	✓	✗	✓	✓	✗	✓	✗	12
Jack Pott	✓	✓	✗	✗	✓	✗	✗	✗	✗	✗	✗	✗	✗	✗	✗	✗	✗	3
Jacolyn Hyde	✗	✓	✗	✗	✗	✗	✗	✗	✗	✗	✓	✗	✗	✗	✗	✓	✗	3
Leigh King	✓	✓	✓	✓	✓	✗	✓	✓	✓	✓	✓	✓	✗	✓	✓	✓	✓	15
Moe Skeeto	✓	✗	✓	✗	✓	✓	✗	✗	✗	✗	✓	✓	✗	✓	✓	✓	✗	9
Noah Lott	✓	✓	✓	✓	✓	✓	✓	✓	✗	✗	✓	✗	✓	✓	✗	✗	✓	12
Sarah Bellum	✓	✓	✓	✗	✓	✓	✓	✓	✓	✗	✓	✗	✓	✓	✓	✓	✓	14
Sue Render	✓	✓	✓	✓	✓	✓	✓	✓	✓	✓	✓	✓	✓	✓	✓	✓	✓	17

Figure 5.1 Mark book example.

The problem with stopping at this point is that it does not really tell us much about what the learner knows and is ready to learn next, nor does it provide us with any information about the quality of our evidence. We can use any spreadsheet program to help us organise our data to evaluate the quality of our evidence by using the sorting functions. Figure 5.2 shows the same set of class data that has been arranged to create a **Guttman chart** (also known as a scalogram). Students have been sorted according to their score (highest score at the top, lowest score at the bottom) and the items, or questions, have been arranged from the easiest (the question with the greatest number of correct responses) to the most difficult (the question with the lowest number of correct responses). To learn more about creating Guttman charts there are many online resources available to take you through each step.

Through this simple transformation, we are already able to make judgements using this data. It is clear that for the first four students listed, the assessment task was too easy. We have not learnt much about what they need to learn next. The assessment had a ceiling effect for these students. But what about the questions they got wrong? Heidi missed Question 5, which is one of the easier questions, so this was probably a lapse in concentration, perhaps a forgotten unit of measurement in her response. Likewise, Leigh and Gene were able to answer more difficult questions correctly. This is where knowing your students and the context is important, as you will quickly be able to

Student	2	3	1	5	14	16	7	11	6	15	8	17	12	9	13	4	10	Raw score
Sue Render	1	1	1	1	1	1	1	1	1	1	1	1	1	1	1	1	1	17
Gene Poole	1	1	1	1	1	1	1	1	1	1	0	1	1	1	1	1	1	16
Heidi Clare	1	1	1	0	1	1	1	1	1	1	1	1	1	1	1	1	1	16
Leigh King	1	1	1	1	1	1	1	1	0	1	1	1	1	1	0	1	1	15
Doris Schutt	1	1	1	1	1	1	1	1	1	1	1	1	0	0	1	1	0	14
Sarah Bellum	1	1	1	1	1	1	1	1	1	1	1	1	0	1	1	0	0	14
Adam Zapel	1	1	1	1	1	1	1	0	1	1	0	1	1	0	1	0	1	13
Al Dente	1	1	1	1	1	1	1	1	0	1	1	1	1	0	1	0	0	13
Cara Van	1	1	1	1	1	1	1	0	1	1	1	1	1	0	0	0	0	12
Hugh Morris	1	1	1	1	1	1	1	1	1	0	0	0	0	1	1	1	0	12
Noah Lott	1	1	1	1	1	0	1	1	1	0	1	1	0	0	1	1	0	12
Barb Dwyer	1	1	0	1	0	1	1	0	0	1	1	0	1	1	0	0	0	9
Alf A. Romeo	1	1	1	0	1	1	0	1	1	0	0	0	1	1	0	0	0	9
Moe Skeeto	0	1	1	1	1	1	0	1	1	1	0	0	1	0	0	0	0	9
B.A. Ware	1	1	1	1	0	1	1	1	0	0	1	0	0	0	0	1	0	9
Ali Gaither	0	1	1	1	1	0	0	0	0	0	0	0	0	1	0	0	0	5
Carrie Oakey	1	1	1	1	0	0	1	0	0	0	0	0	0	0	0	0	0	5
Earl E. Bird	1	0	0	1	1	0	0	0	0	0	1	0	0	0	0	0	0	4
Jack Pott	1	0	1	1	0	0	0	0	0	0	0	0	0	0	0	0	0	3
Jacolyn Hyde	1	0	0	0	0	1	0	1	0	0	0	0	0	0	0	0	0	3
No. of correct responses	18	17	17	17	15	15	14	13	11	11	11	10	10	9	9	8	5	

Figure 5.2 Guttman chart example.

identify if the error is a minor gap that can be quickly and easily addressed, or a lapse in concentration. Either way, these students have demonstrated mastery of the construct. If we look to Ali's pattern of responses, we can see that Ali's score of 5 included one of the more difficult responses. Based on this, it would be a reasonable assumption that Ali had a lucky guess with Question 9. We can also use our Guttman chart to consider whether or not the performance of any student or item is quality evidence. If we look at Barb's pattern of responses, we observe a pattern of ones and zeros across the entire assessment. What we expect to see in a Guttman is a breakdown in the pattern of ones and zeros as students reach their zone of proximal development as items become more difficult for them. Barb doesn't have a pattern of ones, followed by zeros, rather they are sprinkled across easier and harder questions, which does not make sense. Context matters here. It could be that Barb was sick that day or had other concerns that impacted her ability to concentrate. Speaking with Barb and drawing on what the teacher knows about her will be key to understanding why this unusual pattern of responses occurred. Regardless, this is a good example of poor-quality evidence and should be ruled inadmissible as evidence of learning for this learner.

We can apply the same standard to the performance of items or questions. There is an expectation that we see a pattern of ones, followed by zeros as we move down the chart. Those with higher levels of competence are more likely to respond correctly, and therefore there should be a breakdown in ones. Item 8 is an example of an item that doesn't appear to be performing as expected. In other words, those with lower levels of competence are able to respond correctly, and those with higher levels are responding incorrectly. This indicates that the question is perhaps worded ambiguously and does not serve its function to discriminate between learners and their current level of development. A decision would need to be made as to whether Question 8 was included in any decisions made about teaching and learning based on its questionable performance.

When we look at overall patterns, it is also possible to determine if there is inherent bias in the assessment. To check this, do not just review individual students and items, also consider if there are 'groups' of students who have perhaps underperformed on a specific item or set of items. This bias may be gender-based, cultural, language-based, etc. If there is a pattern, then the assessment item or perhaps the assessment itself is likely to be biased in that it is more difficult for some students than others based on the design of the task that is separate from their ability.

For those interested in psychometrics, this approach is related to probabilistic models and can be extended by using **Item Response Theory**, such as **Rasch modelling**, to extend the analysis even further and develop a more nuanced understanding of the data. This discussion is beyond the scope of this book but if interested in learning more about this, there are many resources available.

How do we interpret evidence?

Once we have collected evidence of student learning, there needs to be a frame of reference upon which we make claims and judgements based on this evidence. We need a way of understanding what the evidence means in a broader context and how we can use it to make informed decisions.

Three common interpretive frameworks are norm-referenced, standards-referenced and criterion-referenced. These were discussed in Chapter 3 in the context of tests and are summarised in Table 5.1.

Knowing how evidence from assessment tasks will be interpreted should be determined at the planning stage. For standardised assessments, this will already be prescribed as per the administration instructions. But for criterion- and standards-referenced assessments, there needs to be consideration of what the evidence looks like, that is what students will make, see, do and write.

Developing an assessment framework will provide the details of the evidence of learning for the skills and knowledge we want to assess. The assessment framework, including assessment criteria, both explains and clarifies expectations of the task and shows what development looks like, but can also encourage and limit engagement with the task.[1] It is proposed that assessment criteria serve a role in 'inviting' to act: to provide a 'productive space,' to sustain learning and to reflect on their learning.[2]

Table 5.1 Common interpretive frameworks

Interpretative framework	Description	Purpose	Example
Norm-referenced	Compare an individual's performance to a predefined group, often called the 'norm group.' This group is a representative sample of a larger population for which the assessment is intended. The main questions norm-referenced interpretations aim to answer include how an individual's performance stacks up against peers or what percentile rank an individual holds within a larger group.	To classify and rank individuals relative to one another within a large group.	Standardised tests like ICAS, PAT assessments and IQ tests where scores are reported as percentile ranks.
Criterion-referenced	Evaluate an individual's performance against a specific set of criteria or learning standards, rather than comparing scores to those of other individuals. This type of assessment is focused on determining whether an individual has achieved mastery or proficiency in a particular skill or knowledge area.	To assess individual level of development in skill and/or knowledge areas, useful for understanding current level of mastery and instructional needs.	Using a rubric to assess an oral presentation or project.
Standards-referenced	Align with detailed learning standards defined by educational authorities or professional organisations. These standards outline what students are expected to learn at specific grade levels or after completing certain courses. Standards-based assessments aim to ensure that all students meet these predetermined learning goals.	To ensure that instruction and assessment are aligned with educational standards, focusing on what students should know and be able to do at various stages of their education.	End-of-unit/semester tests that assess students' mastery of state or national educational standards in subjects like Mathematics and English.

To unpack this further, this means assessment criteria should[3]

- Provide detail yet allow for student interpretation free from constraints (ceiling effects).
- Provide boundaries but allow for students to contribute their own ideas within those boundaries.

- Promote deeper learning through engaging in a productive space, rather than assessing against fixed norms.
- Be applicable across multiple assessment opportunities to promote continued learning and development.
- Support development through student exploration and interpretation of assessment criteria beyond the 'right answer.'

How do we achieve such invitational criteria? The key lies in understanding the learning progression as they identify and map how the learning develops within a given construct. If we know what development 'looks' like, then we can use this to inform our planning and assessment practices. Progressions can also be referred to as construct maps. The Australian Curriculum provides learning progressions for Literacy and Numeracy, which are further delineated into elements (e.g., speaking and listening, reading and viewing, number sense and algebra).[4]

Progressions describe how development proceeds and the levels of competence that characterise that development. Theories of skill acquisition, such as the Dreyfus and Dreyfus model of skill acquisition,[5] provide a way of thinking about this progression through the following levels of skill development. Each level can be described using typical patterns of behaviour.

1 **Novice**: beginners with no experience who rely on rules/guidelines to achieve tasks have a superficial level of understanding. They do not tend to deviate from the 'rules' or instructions.
2 **Advanced beginner**: has some experience and can recognise contextual elements and applies guidelines with consideration of the specific context. They draw on basic principles but still rely on rules to act.
3 **Competent:** will be more involved in their learning process drawing on their experience. They consider long-term goals and can plan their actions accordingly and draw on patterns.
4 **Proficient:** has a deep understanding of the skill area and can intuitively understand what needs to be done based on a holistic view of the situation. They learn from their experiences and can adjust their performance based on their insights.
5 **Expert:** has extensive experience and knowledge facilitating actions based on intuition. They operate in a fluid, somewhat 'effortless' manner. They no longer rely on rules or guidelines and often can't explain the 'why' behind decision-making.

If you think about an area of knowledge or skills that you have experience with, whether as a teacher or a learner, reflect on how this model applies to the stages of development in that context. It may be writing a narrative or developing algebraic understanding, learning how to play tennis or learning how to drive a car. How many times have you arrived at your destination as a driver and wondered how you got there? The decision-making and actions you took as an experienced driver can become second nature – we do it without having to think about it too much. Until, perhaps, we switch to a European car or vice versa and have windscreen wipers going when wanted to indicate a left-hand turn!

When applying this model and thinking about what different levels of development 'look' like, draw on your own expertise and experience with learners and what you have seen in the past. What are the features of a narrative that is executed? What are the features of a narrative of a novice writer? From our own classroom experience, apart from endings like 'and then I woke up. It was all a dream,' or some catastrophic explosion, novice authors may list events of the story. The events may be separate from each other. Characters will be named. They rely on familiar openings and endings as a 'formula' for writing. As the writer develops their competence, the characters become more developed and complex. The arc of the narrative is crafted to engage the reader. The writing elicits an emotional response. Word choice and sentence structure are considered with deliberate selections. By drawing on what students do, say, make and write at different levels of development, as well as referring to curriculum documents and any other relevant sources, teachers locate students' development on the progression, plan for teaching and learning, share with students for goal setting and develop appropriate assessment criteria.

A possible progression for writing narratives could be:

Level 5	Learners create sophisticated character arcs and immersive worlds that are integral to the mood, themes and conflicts of the story. They develop complex plots with multiple layers, integrating intricate subplots and nuanced themes that reflect real-world issues or human experiences. This level is marked by exceptional storytelling skills, with students capable of creating rich, nuanced narratives that resonate with readers on multiple levels, showcasing their full range of narrative writing abilities.
Level 4	Learners refine their narrative techniques by focusing on dynamic character development, where characters grow or learn lessons and by exploring rich setting details that immerse the reader in the story's world. The introduction of subplots enriches the narrative, and themes or messages begin to take shape, offering deeper meaning to the stories. Learners use descriptive language and detail skillfully, creating complex plots and character arcs that engage readers.
Level 3	Learners create more complex stories by developing characters with depth, including their emotions and motivations, and detailing settings with rich descriptions. The plots become more intricate, incorporating minor events that build towards a climax and demonstrate cause and effect. Conflict and resolution become key components, as learners demonstrate how characters face and overcome challenges. There is creative use of language and structure, enabling students to craft engaging stories that show a clear sequence of events and a heightened sense of climax.

Level 2	Learners start to enhance their descriptions of characters and settings. They begin to add sensory details to describe where and when stories take place, alongside beginning to describe characters' looks, actions and feelings. Students learn to create simple stories that have a clear sequence, introducing the concept of conflict as a driving force in narratives.
Level 1	Learners are immersed in the basic elements of narrative writing. They begin to understand stories as sequences of events, recognising the fundamental structure that includes a beginning, middle and end. Students begin to understand that stories involve individuals who experience events in particular places and times.

With our progressions in hand, we now have a map of what to look for and how to target teaching. The next step is to develop assessment criteria that allow for valid and reliable judgements to be made. We advocate for developmental criterion-reference rubrics as they have the capacity to evaluate the progression of skills or competencies over time. Instead of just outlining performance criteria and levels of achievement, developmental rubrics include multiple progression levels that represent stages of skill development or mastery.[6] These levels may be based on a continuum from novice to expert or may reflect incremental steps of improvement. Because of these features, they facilitate the invitational propositions for assessment criteria described earlier in this chapter.

Rubrics

We remember being introduced to rubrics as beginning teachers. It made so much sense to be able to mark student work in such a manner that provides both a score and feedback. The term 'rubric' derives from the Latin word *ruber*, which means 'red,' and originally referred to the red-inked comments or instructions that were added to a manuscript.[7]

In discussing assessment, reliability and validity are unavoidable companions. We know that for the assessment of student learning, we need reliability. Reliability requires judgements that are made consistently over time, tasks and raters (markers). How we interpret or mark evidence of student learning will contribute to the reliability of the assessment.

Rubrics provide a way of enhancing reliability, particularly when the focus of the rubric is on the skills rather than the elements of the task. When a scoring guide focuses on the aspects of the task it makes comparisons over time and tasks difficult. Consider a Geography assessment on landforms that asks about a specific region based on an excursion. It is unlikely that this specific knowledge will be revisited for students to show consistency.

A quality rubric is a scoring guide that defines the criteria for evaluating learner development in a way that is consistent, understandable, aligned with the learning and assessment design, transparent and focused on the construct being assessed. This applies to both behavioural and academic development.

Criterion-referenced rubrics are used to evaluate the quality of performance based on a set of predetermined criteria or standards. In contrast to norm-referenced assessment, where performance is compared to that of other individuals, criterion-referenced assessment focuses on whether specific objectives or criteria have been met.

Qualities of a rubric

As with any assessment tool, there can be 'good' and 'bad' rubrics. We classify good rubrics as rubrics that are useful for teachers and learners alike and can be used to inform and guide learning through quality evidence.

We propose that quality rubrics are:

- **Consistent**: A rubric should be clear and concise so that both students and markers can easily understand the criteria for each performance level. This will help to ensure that students are being assessed fairly and consistently, regardless of who is doing the grading.
- **Understandable**: The criteria in a rubric should be written in language that is clear and easy to understand for both students and markers. This means avoiding jargon and technical terms that may not be familiar to everyone.
- **Aligned with the learning and assessment task**: The criteria in a rubric should be aligned with the learning objectives of the assignment or assessment task. This means that the criteria should focus on the specific skills and/or knowledge that students are expected to demonstrate the targeted construct (e.g., community-building).
- **Transparent**: A rubric should be transparent so that students and markers can see how their work will be assessed. This means that the criteria and performance levels should be clearly explained in the rubric.
- **Focused on the construct**: The criteria in a rubric should be focused on the construct being assessed. This means that the criteria should focus on the underlying knowledge, skills or abilities that students are expected to demonstrate.

Anatomy of a rubric

There are many different rubrics and many different ways of describing them including analytic rubrics, holistic rubrics, task-specific or general.[8] This section provides an overview of the anatomy of developmental rubrics and defines key terms based on the work out of the Assessment Research Centre led by Patrick Griffin.[9]

This approach deviates from the typical horizontal rubric often used for assessment and proposes a vertical presentation that reflects the progression of learning. Figure 5.3 is an excerpt of a rubric for Critical Thinking that was developed by students, teachers and industry partners in a school. The initial development work was led by a group of students who researched the nominated suite of competencies, including curriculum documents, to determine an initial set of *sub-capabilities* (i.e., sets of skills, knowledge) that were required for each competency. In this example, the development team determined that the ability to reason, construct knowledge and make decisions were key components of thinking critically.

Once the capabilities were identified, the group turned their attention to identifying the indicative behaviours (i.e., indicators) that demonstrated reasoning, knowledge construction and decision-making. In this case, the indicators included using logic, analysing, reflecting, using information, asking questions and making judgements. At this point, this is just a list of the behaviours, or things people need to 'do' to think critically as determined by this school for their setting. There is no level of quality attached to these indicative behaviours. If we think back to our painters from Chapter 2, at this point we are just describing the actions required, e.g., sanding, cleaning, patching, filling, sanding again and painting one coat.

This is where the quality criteria come into play as they provide the descriptions that allow judgements to be made about 'how well' the indicative behaviours have been demonstrated. For many rubrics, quality criteria are often written with a reliance on adjectives and adverbs to make the distinction. For our narrative writing, there might be an indicator about the beginning of the narrative that is differentiated by phrases like "A sophisticated opening expertly engaging the reader" and "A well-structured opening" through to "A good opening showing awareness of the reader." You get the idea. We often rely on adjectives like 'excellent,' 'well-developed,' 'sound' and 'developing' to determine levels of quality, but how well are these terms understood? We have been in moderation meetings where interpretation of these types of criteria was described as 'using intuition.' This is alarming on many fronts, as it questions the ability of different markers to apply the criteria consistently across a cohort of students. And if it is not transparent for the teachers, it can't possibly be clear for the students.

Consider the following criteria that could appear in any rubric for an academic task:

- Good use of writing conventions, mostly accurate spelling and grammar, and evidence of proofreading and editing in all documentation. (4 marks)
- Writing conventions followed with small errors, very few spelling or grammar errors and evidence of proofreading and editing in all documentation. (3 marks)

Take a moment to read through these carefully and look for substantive differences. In other words, although different words are used, how does the inherent meaning change? We suggest that it does not and that savvy students being marked on this criterion would have a case to challenge if they were scored a 3. What is the difference between very few errors and 'mostly accurate'? Does not mostly accurate imply 'very few errors'?

Often, we fall into the trap of using words to make criteria 'sound' different, but upon closer inspection, we have really just played word games and the inherent meaning remains the same. Adopting a developmental approach to developing quality criteria forces our hand to break habits of using ambiguous language to differentiate between levels of performance as it demands clarity about what students do, make and write. Griffin and Francis[10] recommend using taxonomies such as Bloom's (cognitive), SOLO (depth of knowledge) and Krathwohl (affective) as a way of structuring increasing complexity that requires increasing levels of competence. These taxonomies have lists of verbs that are representative of levels of complexity that are freely accessible on the internet. It is the selection and use of these verbs in writing criteria that create the distinction between levels of quality (competence).

For example, it is easier to **list** a range of literary devices, for example, metaphor, simile, analogy and personification than it is to **apply** or even **critique** the use of such devices in a piece of writing. By using verbs at the start of each criterion, we are building in different levels of quality without relying on adjectives and adverbs, counts or pseudo counts (e.g., some, many, few).

There are a set of principles for developing effective criteria to consistently measure various responses or performances. These guidelines have evolved through assessment research and psychometric theory and are as follows:[11]

1 **Avoid quantitative counts:** Using numerical counts can discourage students from pushing their boundaries for fear of making mistakes or decreasing accuracy.
2 **Eliminate ambiguous language**: Avoid subjective descriptors like 'good' or 'suitable,' which can cause inconsistency as people bring their own interpretation of these terms.
3 **Steer clear of procedural steps**: Criteria based on completing procedural steps may overlook the quality of each step and performance will be marked on how many steps were completed rather than how well.
4 **Progressive performance levels**: Descriptions should clearly delineate increasing levels of performance, utilising developmental taxonomies (e.g., Bloom's, SOLO, Krathwohl or Fink's Significant Learning[12]) to highlight substantive differences in quality.
5 **Focus on a single idea:** Criteria should concentrate on one central concept to facilitate clear judgements. Often, we combine many ideas in one criterion which requires markers to assign a weight to each idea when one part is demonstrated and another is not.
6 **Provide observable criteria**: Assessments should be based on direct observations (i.e., what learners do, say, make and write), avoiding negative language to provide clear, actionable feedback.
7 **Cover a range of levels of competence:** Rubrics should challenge students at all levels, from beginners to the most proficient, encouraging all to stretch their abilities.

8 **Avoid weightings**: Criterion-referenced assessments should not use weightings, allowing for direct teaching adjustments based on assessment data.
9 **Limit the number of criteria per indicator**: To ensure consistent judgements, restrict the number of criteria per indicator, simplifying distinctions between quality levels. Aim for no more than four criteria.
10 **Maintain transparency:** Criteria should be clear and jargon-free, enabling students to understand and engage with their assessment process and increasing reliability across markers.

If you review the excerpt in Figure 5.3, you will see how these principles can be enacted to create a clear assessment tool. However, the clarity of the tool still relies on phrasing and an understanding of the verbs used. This is not a silver bullet and it cannot be assumed that students and markers will immediately understand and use the rubric. As with all things teaching and learning, any rubric should be introduced to students and time taken to unpack what is

	1.1	1.2	2.1	2.2	2.3	3.1
Quality criteria		1.2.3 Applies the connections among components (parts) to construct an argument or reach a conclusion	2.1.3 Evaluates own thinking (e.g., identifies assumptions and bias)	2.2.3 Evaluates/Justifies credibility of information from different sources	2.3.4 Asks critical questions (e.g., How do we know this is true? Why is this important?)	3.1.4 Explains judgement based on comparing things similar in their nature
	1.1.2 Constructs arguments using deductive reasoning (i.e., All dogs have 4 legs. My pet is a dog. My pet has 4 legs)			2.2.2 Synthesises information from different sources	2.3.3 Asks evaluative questions (e.g., What makes this a good book?)	3.1.3 Explains judgement based on criteria
		1.2.2 Describes the relationship between the parts (e.g., similarities, groupings)	2.1.2 Explains own thinking		2.3.2 Asks inquiring questions (e.g., Why do you think this is the case? What sort of impact do you think...?)	3.1.2 Explains judgement based on rules or generalisations
	1.1.1 Uses simple conditional statements (e.g., if/then)	1.2.1 Identifies elements or parts	2.1.1 Describes own thinking (e.g., mindmaps, shows working out)	2.2.1 Identifies facts and opinions	2.3.1 Asks factual or closed questions (e.g., What is the square root of four?)	3.1.1 States likes and dislikes
	Insufficient evidence	Insufficient evidence	Insufficient evidence	Insufficient evidence	Insufficient evidence	Insufficient evidence
Indicators	1.1 Using logic	1.2 Analysing	2.1 Reflecting	2.2 Using information	2.3 Asking questions	3.1 Making judgements
Sub-capabilities	1. Reasoning		2. Constructing knowledge			3. Making decisions

Figure 5.3 Critical thinking rubric excerpt.

meant by the criteria and what it might look like in the specific context. Verbs used may require explicit teaching and the use of a glossary of command terms such as these verbs is a valuable tool to have on hand to ensure consistency in interpretation.

A tale of two criteria: Stories from the grading scale

Commonly, rubrics presented horizontally will have four or five columns that may be labelled low, medium, high or strongly meets or exceeds requirements through to does not meet requirements, or sometimes just a number as per the example in Figure 5.4. This excerpt of a rubric in Figure 5.4 rubric is inspired by an example freely available on the internet and represents any number of rubrics that are written in this way. Each box will have a criterion, and there is an assumption that all criteria within that column are the same in terms of quality. For this example, providing a 'catchy' title is scored the same as addressing important elements of a narrative text (introduction, resolution, etc.). Take a moment to review all of the criteria listed presented in this rubric. Most are problematic due to ambiguity and assumptions made about creative licence (e.g., leaving unanswered questions) and determining 'effort.' Aside from this, consider the assigned scores and whether they are all equal in terms of difficulty or level of competence required. Does it make sense to be scored a one for not providing a title or resolution?

This then raises a couple of questions. Firstly, by filling every box with a criterion, we may be forcing a level of quality that is not distinct in its own right. This is about **grain size** (i.e., level of detail and specificity) and can lead to using adjectives to try and create a level when perhaps there is not one. It is better to leave a gap and ensure that there is a discernible difference in quality. This can be a challenging mindset shift as teachers and students alike are not necessarily used to having gaps in a rubric and requires explanation and understanding of this approach.

Secondly, we need to consider the difficulty of each criterion, or the degree of competence required for each criterion. There are ways of empirically measuring this, but we need to start with a hypothetical level of difficulty when we first design our rubrics. These hypothesised levels of difficulty are not a guess but is based on expertise in the learning area and draws on the experience of teachers working with students. To determine these levels of difficulty and subsequent placement in the rubric, compare each criterion with another. Do they require a similar level of ability or is one easier or harder. Looking at the rubric in Figure 5.3, criterion 1.1.2 is positioned higher than criterion 1.2.2. Even though they are both the second criteria listed (and would score a 2), they have been determined to require different levels of competence (ability) to achieve the criterion. This process of comparing criterion has been applied across the rubric and determined the location based on the hypothesised level of difficulty.

As mentioned, there is a way of checking empirically whether these levels are correct. There is psychometric software that can be used to conduct formal statistical analysis using item response theory but it can also be checked

Category	4	3	2	1
Writing process	Student spends significant time and effort into the writing process, working hard to produce a wonderful story.	Student puts in adequate time and effort into the writing process, ensuring the task is completed satisfactorily.	Student allocates a moderate amount of time and effort to the writing process, though the work lacks depth. They do the bare minimum required.	Student shows minimal investment in time and effort towards the writing process, indicating a lack of interest.
Introduction	The first paragraph opens with a strong, engaging hook.	The opening paragraph presents an attempt at a compelling hook but falls short.	An effort was made to create an intriguing start, yet it resulted in confusion rather than engagement.	The first paragraph does not make an effort to captivate the reader's attention.
Spelling and punctuation	The text is free from spelling or punctuation mistakes, with character and place names created by the author being consistently spelled throughout.	The final draft contains a single spelling or punctuation mistake.	The final version has 2 to 3 errors in spelling and punctuation.	There are over three spelling and punctuation errors in the final draft.
Solution /resolution	The resolution to the character's issue is clear and logical, leaving no unanswered questions.	The resolution to the character's dilemma is comprehensible and reasonably logical.	Understanding the solution to the character's problem requires some effort.	Either no resolution is presented, or it does not make sense.
Title	The title is inventive, captures attention, and aligns with the story's theme and content.	The title is related to the story's theme and content.	Title seems unrelated to the story's theme and content.	No title.

Figure 5.4 Example of common rubric (narrative writing).

using a Guttman chart and sorting the items and students as discussed earlier in this chapter. There is an extra step involved as the rubric provides **partial credit data** that needs to be transformed into **dichotomous data**. Once this transformation is done through, it becomes easy to check whether our hypothesised order of difficulty is represented in the data and we can make adjustments accordingly.

Moderation

Moderation is a familiar step in the assessment process as teaching teams meet to review and compare assessments to ensure consistency, fairness and reliability across all markers and learners. This quality assurance process aims to align the marking standards and outcomes, especially when multiple assessors are involved or when a single assessor is evaluating a large set of learners over time.

The moderation process begins pre-assessment with a focus on discussing and reviewing marking criteria (such as rubrics) to ensure teachers have a shared understanding prior to commencing this work with their learners. When developing new rubrics, or using existing ones, reviewing the quality of the rubric at this stage is important to ensure that any evidence of student learning collected via the assessment is quality evidence. We offer a list of characteristics that have been derived from the qualities of a developmental rubric and provide a useful structure for use during pre-assessment moderation to evaluate rubric quality with some tips provided for each.

1 **Is the rubric fit for purpose?** Look for alignment among intended learning outcomes (ILO), instruction and assessment. The assessment goals (i.e., the construct) should be reflected in the indicators.

   TIP: use the ILOs for the assessment task to identify the constructs being assessed. Work through each ILO to identify the underlying skills and knowledge areas (competencies).

   E.g., Assessment task = differentiated lesson plan

   ILO: Differentiate between teaching and intervention approaches that are well-supported by rigorous research evidence and those that are of low efficacy and impact.

   INDICATOR: Uses evidence-based approaches

2 **Does the rubric promote self-regulation?** Indicators and criteria should provide learners with an understanding of the competency that allows them to develop as self-regulated learners.

   TIP: Consider what a novice typically does and what an expert typically does for the indicator. If you have used the task before, think about the features of the best responses and the lower-level responses. Your rubric should provide a description of the next level of competence to guide the learner on how to improve.

   E.g., Indicator: Uses evidence-based approaches
   - Lists evidence-based approaches (novice)
   - Describes evidence-based approaches
   - Justifies evidence-based approaches based on student needs (expert)

3 **Is the rubric developmental and criterion-referenced:** Are criteria representative of the developmental progression of the skill (i.e., behaviours that are increasingly sophisticated)?

TIP: Use a taxonomy to assist with developmental progression. For example, Bloom's, Fink or SOLO for cognitive complexity, Krathwohl for affective behaviour. The Dreyfus & Dreyfus model of skill acquisition level descriptions is also helpful.

4 **Does the rubric allow for consistency of decisions?** Does the language used allow for consistent judgements (no ambiguous language, such as adjectives or adverbs).

TIP: Begin each criterion with a VERB. The distinction between levels lies in the VERB as per the example above, rather than relying on subjective adjectives, counts and pseudo-counts (i.e., sometimes, few, consistently).

E.g., Instead of "very clear description of evidence-based approaches," write 'describes...' To describe something means it has to be clear, or it hasn't been described! The differentiation in *quality* lies in the verb.

5 **Are criteria directly observable?** Indicators and criteria should be written in a way that allows for direct observation of the behaviour.

TIP: What do different qualities of performance 'look' like? We cannot see what someone 'knows.' We want them to show us how they can apply their skills and understanding of the subject. I know in theory how to lay tiles, but if I applied my skills to your bathroom – you would ask for a refund.

6 **Are criteria transparent and invite students to action?** Are criteria written in a way that is understandable for all users of the rubric and allow for deeper learning.

TIP: use clear language and be succinct. Stick to one criterion per 'box' and focus on the core skills and understandings (ILOs). This may mean more 'rows,' but it will be clearer and easier to work with for everyone.

7 **Are there measurable levels of performance:** (grain size) quantity and focus of criteria allow for distinct, measurable, clearly delineated levels of performance that provide a scale for assessing the quality of performance.

TIPS:

No more than four levels of performance. Beyond this, the grain size is too small and making meaningful distinctions is difficult.

If you only have two criteria for an indicator, do not force the split to fill the boxes. Make it dichotomous.

When using verbs to begin your statements, select from different levels of the taxonomy you are using. Ensure all users of the rubric understand the definitions of these command terms. Consider providing a glossary and explicitly teaching the command. For example, teach what it means to synthesise and provide opportunities for students to practice. (Note: potential to consider this from a course-level perspective.)

From drab to fab: A rubric makeover

This section takes the rather questionable rubric for narrative writing in Figure 5.4 and gives it a makeover. Reviewing the rubric based on the information in this chapter would leave it falling short on a number of elements in terms of its usefulness as a tool for assessment, let alone for teaching and learning.

The first thing to consider is the construct, that is narrative writing. We can revisit the progression presented earlier in this chapter to identify the skills, knowledge and understandings required to produce a narrative text.

Narrative writing requires both creative and technical skills, as well as knowledge that supports the author in crafting engaging and coherent stories. Some of the key skills and areas of knowledge include:

- Storytelling skills
- Character development
- Setting and world-building
- Language and style
- Structure
- Dialogue
- Research skills
- Creativity and imagination

These can be grouped into different sub-capabilities of technical skills and creative skills, as shown in Table 5.2. This can provide us with the indicative behaviours that can be included in a rubric.

These could be broken down further into written expression, structure and experimentation. Ultimately, the indicators and the ways in which these are organised will depend on the context and the content experts in the school (i.e., the teaching team).

Once these are decided upon, it is a matter of determining how these manifest differently based on level of development. The rubric offered in Figure 5.5 is *one* way that an English team may develop an assessment instrument that is useful for teaching and learning as well as assessing student work. This is not intended to be a perfect example and would need to be presented to a team of colleagues and students to ensure it made sense and reflected the intended

Table 5.2 Identifying indicators and sub-capabilities for narrative writing

Creative skills	Technical skills
- Engages the audience	- Demonstrates appropriate meta-language
- Develops character	- Uses research skills
- Use of dialogue	- Employs editing
- Develops setting and world-building	- Adheres to genre conventions (e.g., Structure)
- Takes creative risks	

Quality criteria	Adheres to genre conventions (structure)	Develops character	Uses dialogue
	Applies narrative features in novel or unique ways (e.g., begin with a resolution)	Creates meaning through what characters do and say (i.e., dialogue and action)	Applies dialogue to create meaning (e.g., rather than a character stating they are angry, the dialogue shows the character is angry)
	Experiments with structural features (e.g., adding a secondary storyline, foreshadowing or flashbacks)	Connects characters through interaction with others (e.g., how they intersect)	
			Integrates dialogue to enhance story (e.g., dialogue between characters)
		Describes characters through listing actions (i.e., characters do a, then do b)	Connects dialogue to characters
	Draws on familiar narrative structures (e.g., start, middle, end)	Names characters	Lists dialogue in a format similar to that of a play
	Insufficient evidence	Insufficient evidence	Insufficient evidence
Indicators	**Adheres to genre conventions (structure)**	**Develops character**	**Uses dialogue**
Sub-capabilities	**Technical skills**	**Creative skills**	

Figure 5.5 Excerpt of developmental rubric for narrative writing.

learning objectives. It would also need to be revised after its first use depending on whether its criteria work or do not work as expected.

Developing these rubrics takes time and practice. It is easier to think about differences in quality through deficits and adjectives. The mindset shift to identify the underlying skills, knowledge, etc. of what we want students to learn and develop requires more effort. This is true of any change to ways of working that may have become embedded practice and to some degree, second nature. In teaching, time is a valuable commodity. Our recommendation for starting this work is to start small with like-minded colleagues and just give it a go. Discussions with students and colleagues should quickly prove the effort is worth it as there is greater clarity, reliability and validity in what is being measured, not just for summative purposes but also to give evidence of learning that can be used for future teaching and learning.

Chapter summary and reflection

This chapter has focused on ensuring the collection of evidence of learning yields useable, quality information that can be used by both learners and educators. One way of checking for quality evidence is through using Guttman charts that sort assessment data into a visual format that allows for easy identification of evidence that should be disregarded or retained. Different ways of interpreting the evidence, including standards-, criterion- and norm-referenced, were explained. Knowing and understanding how the skills and knowledge areas develop and are evidenced were key focuses of this chapter to ensure quality evidence and measurement tools, such as rubrics, are fit for purpose. This means that they not only assess what we want students to learn but also provide students and teachers with valuable information about 'where to next.' The ideas and approaches presented in this chapter may require a mindset shift for some teachers, which can initially be challenging and takes time and practice. Whilst this is something individual teachers can do on their own, this process really requires, and benefits from, a team of colleagues working together to bounce ideas off each other and draw on the collective expertise when considering how the construct develops or typically progresses. The time and effort are worthwhile as the rubrics you create become much more than tools for providing a score on an assessment but are maps for teaching and learning as well. Tips for reviewing rubrics as part of a pre-assessment moderation process were provided.

To help consolidate and consider how you can implement the key ideas in this chapter, reflect on the following questions:

1 After reading this chapter, how has your understanding of rubrics changed?
2 Identify an existing rubric you use for marking student work – how can this rubric can be improved?
3 With a team, construct new rubrics that reflect the understandings in this chapter for an upcoming unit/topic.

Notes

1 Bearman, M., & Ajjawi, R. (2021). Can a rubric do more than be transparent? Invitation as a new metaphor for assessment criteria. *Studies in Higher Education*, *46*(2), 359–368. https://doi.org/10.1080/03075079.2019.1637842.

2 Ibid.

3 Ibid.

4 Australian Curriculum, Assessment and Reporting Authority. (n.d.). *National literacy and numeracy learning progressions.* https://www.australiancurriculum.edu. au/resources/national-literacy-and-numeracy-learning-progressions/.

5 Rousse, B., & Dreyfus, S. (2021). Revisiting the six stages of skill acquisition. In Elaine M. Silva Mangiante, Jane Northup, Kathy Peno (Eds.), *Teaching and learning for adult skill acquisition: Applying the Dreyfus & Dreyfus model in different fields* (pp. 3–28). Information Age Publishing.

6 Griffin, P., & Francis, M. (2017). Writing rubrics. In P. Griffin (Ed.), *Assessment for teaching* (2nd ed., pp. 113–140). Cambridge University Press. https://doi. org/10.1017/9781108116053.008.

7 Merriam-Webster. (n.d.). *Rubric.* In Merriam-Webster.com dictionary. Retrieved 29 February 2024, from https://www.merriam-webster.com/dictionary/rubric.

8 Dawson, P. (2017). Assessment rubrics: Towards clearer and more replicable design, research and practice. *Assessment & Evaluation in Higher Education, 42*(3), 347–360. https://doi.org/10.1080/02602938.2015.1111294.

9 Griffin, P., & Francis, M. (2017). Writing rubrics. In P. Griffin (Ed.), *Assessment for teaching* (2nd ed., pp. 113–140). Cambridge University Press. https://doi. org/10.1017/9781108116053.008.

10 Ibid.

11 Ibid.

12 Fink, L.D. (2013). *Creating significant learning experiences: An integrated approach to designing college courses.* John Wiley & Sons.

6 Co-constructed assessment

What does it mean to be an active learner in the assessment process? Many educators would argue that we should involve students in the learning process, as students should take ownership of their learning. However, when we consider what the role of students should be in assessment, there is often a range of perspectives on how much we can and should involve students in assessment design and assessment processes. Assessment is often traditionally viewed as a key responsibility of the teacher, with some teachers having concerns that if students are involved in the design and/or judgements about their performance, it will compromise validity and objectivity. This way of thinking about assessment is not only observed in teacher practice in schools but is widely accepted outside of the classroom. For example, a US representative for California and law professor, Katie Porter, used an assessment example to argue, at a House Natural Resources Committee hearing, that organisations should not be able to conduct their own environmental reviews without appropriate oversight:

> If you could give yourself a grade, what grade would you give yourself on your performance today? I think most people would give themselves an 'A.' That was always my experience as a professor when I let my students grade themselves.[1]

While Representative Porter is arguing that oversight (e.g., that of a teacher or a regulative body) is needed to ensure that an assessment or evaluation of performance is valid, this example highlights some of the common misconceptions that relate to students' involvement in assessment. This chapter aims to first identify and counter some of these misconceptions that commonly shape our understanding of students' involvement in the assessment process.

Addressing the misconceptions

Students would struggle to provide an honest account of their performance. There is the misconception that if students were given the chance to assign their own grades or marks, they would give themselves the highest mark possible

DOI: 10.4324/9781032657219-6

rather than one that reflects their performance. They would do this because they have an opportunity to take advantage of the situation for their own benefit. There is evidence in higher education contexts that when students' self-assessment marks contribute to their overall grade or mark, there is a tendency for students to rate themselves higher than external markers.[2] However, when assessments are used formatively and are oriented towards development and learning rather than final marks, there is evidence that self-assessment scores from students are more aligned to those of external markers.[3]

This misconception that students would struggle to provide an honest account of their performance, which is held by some but not all educators, speaks to how much we trust students. While in the past we have had **honour systems** that recognise that students will follow rules and can be trusted, increasingly there is a distrust within schools that students will do the right thing. Can we trust students to be honest about their performance, particularly if there are not concurrent assessment tasks to validate or corroborate students' self-assessment scores? This mindset is grounded in the notion that assessment is fair when it is standardised, objective and accurate and having students self-assign their own marks seems widely out of step with this approach as opportunities are opened for students to 'take advantage' of their newly found assessment power. Interestingly, this notion of trust can go both ways, particularly in trusting the decision-making power of others. Teachers must also take intentional steps to ensure that they are assessing reliably by using a range of strategies to ensure that they have clear guidelines of what they are assessing and appropriate levels of performance that clearly define performance from novice to expert. Similarly, if teachers are concerned that students might not provide honest representations of their own performance, then we need to consider how to ensure that the self-assessment instruments and processes that we have introduced might be adapted to provide more accurate and honest evaluations.

Students do not have the skills or understanding (expertise) to assess their work. Another misconception that can shape educators' decision-making regarding the involvement of students in the assessment process is their perception of their students' ability or competence to assess their own work. Research suggests that some teachers do not involve their students in the assessment process because they do not feel they have the ability or competence to do so.[4] While this promotes a deficit view of students, which we do not advocate for or support, this research captures the actual perspectives of teachers regarding how they view their students. Additionally, there is evidence that the accuracy of student self-assessments is often reduced with younger students and those who are less academically proficient.[5,6,7] Therefore, there is empirical evidence to suggest that the accuracy of students' self-assessments is not always good because they may not have the knowledge, skills or expertise to accurately assess their work. However, we argue that accuracy does not have to be the main focus of the self-assessment but that students can learn and gain insights through the process of self-assessment as they reflect on their learning. Furthermore, if the role of the teacher is to develop knowledge, skills and expertise among their students, then teachers must do more to support students in understanding how to self-assess their work. If students' accuracy in their self-assessment is a priority – and note that we would argue that it does not need to be – then educators should view self-assessment as a competency that can be explicitly taught, modelled, scaffolded and assessed over time.

Unlike the previous misconception, in which students have a good sense of their ability but exaggerate their performance to advantage themselves, this misconception is grounded in teachers' lack of confidence in students' ability to self-assess their work. However, we often forget that if teachers want to develop students' knowledge or skills in a particular area, then they will need to plan for, teach and assess this. Competencies are not automatically developed but must be planned, taught and assessed. Self-assessment is no different. If we want to build students' capacity to self-assess, we need to explicitly teach, model and allow them multiple opportunities to self-assess their work.

Teachers need to be the regulator or the decision-maker. While quality teachers are hailed as the key to student success, when national test scores are in decline, teachers are often blamed for their lack of knowledge, expertise and competence.[8] Ultimately, there is a lot of pressure on teachers to demonstrate they have the ability and oversight to ensure strong student outcomes. This can create tension for many educators as they feel they have to continually prove their ability and expertise throughout their initial teacher education degree and their careers.[9] It is those demeaning statements that we have all heard that often shape perceptions of teaching: "Those who can't do, teach!" or "Teachers have it easy with long holidays and short working hours". While misguided, these statements fuel the need for educators to demonstrate their expertise and ensure that they are accountable to students, parents, the school and the broader community. In addition, many teachers attempt to tightly control how they assess student learning, as this is where they will most likely be held accountable.

So, if we consider Representative Porter's comments made earlier, it makes sense for a regulatory body, such as teachers, to verify student learning, especially given that this is their job. However, as discussed before, we assess for different purposes – and we should assess frequently. We just need to ensure that this idea of having oversight – or *insight* – into students' learning and assessment processes is not just about controlling their involvement and limiting their decision-making but that it is about *creating the conditions* and *providing access* to the knowledge, skills and tools needed for students to actively participate in the assessment process.

Once we understand some of the underlying misconceptions that shape our understanding of students' involvement in the assessment process, it is important to consider ways to address and counter these misconceptions:

1 **Clear and consistent assessment instruments.** Before we can question the accuracy of students' self-assessment abilities, we need to make sure

that the self-assessment instruments (e.g., rubrics and checklists) that they are using and/or processes that are undertaken are clear and consistent. Commonly, we have students self-assessing their performance on rubrics that contain criteria they may not understand. One way to ensure that students understand what is being assessed and how to place themselves on a continuum of learning is to carefully go through the rubric with the students and provide clear examples of what the different statements might look like at different levels of performance in the context of the learning area. Teachers can then have students self-assess by determining where they are on the learning continuum, while also providing explicit and clear evidence of their performance for different criteria and indicators. Therefore, teachers must first ensure that rubrics and/or self-assessment instruments are clear and accessible for students and that suitable examples have been provided to demonstrate what each criterion and indicator looks like (see Chapter 5). In addition, teachers can check students' understanding of the criteria and identify what comes next by asking them to provide evidence or examples of their performance to back up their self-assessment. This provides not only accountability but supports students' understanding of how they are addressing the criteria and provides opportunities for student agency.

2 **Development of self-assessment skills.** In addition to ensuring that self-assessment instruments are clear and consistent, both teachers and students need to develop their ability to teach and learn, respectively, the skills related to self-assessment. For example, students would need to develop their ability to reflect on their learning and identify and recognise strengths, weaknesses and future actions that can be taken to improve. Part of this development would also require students to learn how to set goals and evaluate their progress in reaching those goals. Teachers, therefore, would need to facilitate opportunities for students to set goals, reflect, evaluate and identify steps for improvement. To do this, teachers need to explicitly teach what goal setting, planning and reflection look like, while also modelling what this looks like in a classroom environment. This requires building in time and space to assess students' ability to self-assess and then provide targeted feedback and guidance.

3 **Frequency matters.** Given that students should be given multiple opportunities to demonstrate their learning, they should also be given frequent opportunities to be involved in the assessment process. If students had more of a regular say or were given more choices about what should be assessed and how, particularly on formative, low-stakes assessments, they might engage more meaningfully with the assessment process (see Chapter 4). Involving students in the assessment process cannot be limited to allowing students to provide some feedback or complete a self-assessment task once or twice in the year. Rather, it requires a more intentional plan over time that requires examining the routines of the class to determine opportunities to invite students into the assessment process. This approach supports the development of self-assessment, as a competency. Students

are given multiple opportunities over time to learn and demonstrate their ability to self-assess as opportunities to set goals, reflect and plan action are embedded in classroom practices and routines.

Student participation, voice and agency

Chapter 4 explored the concept of student engagement by focusing on the different dimensions of engagement (behavioural, cognitive, emotional and agentic). These dimensions provide insight into students' learning experiences or ways in which they respond and interact with the learning environment. These dimensions are helpful for educators to understand and plan for different ways to maximise student engagement by creating learning environments that can describe and track student engagement. However, when we discuss student engagement, other concepts are often used to describe the different levels in which students are involved in their learning, such as **student participation**, **student voice** and student agency (introduced in Chapter 4). While these concepts also reflect student engagement, they focus on the levels of student *involvement*, *expression* and *autonomy*, respectively, that students actively *choose* to engage with at different points within their learning (see Figure 6.1). Students make choices every day about how they will engage in their learning, with a focus on these three levels of active engagement:

- *participating* in educational processes and activities,
- *having a say* about education matters and
- *taking charge of their learning*.

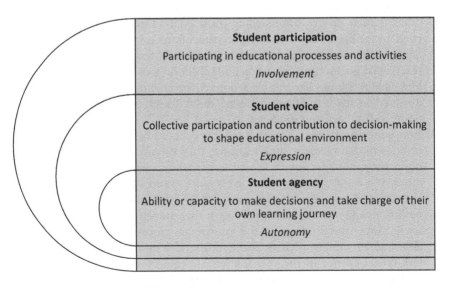

Figure 6.1 Student roles within student engagement.

We view student participation, voice and agency as distinct ways in which students *choose* to engage with the learning process/context. We do not view these roles as a linear process that sees the student start with 'participation' and graduate to 'agency' but recognise that students make choices and move between these roles at different times to respond to different situations. The distinction between this and the dimensions of engagement (i.e., behavioural, cognitive, emotional, agentic) is that student participation, voice and agency describe the extent to which they choose to be active participants, while engagement describes students' engagement experiences. Unfortunately, while teachers can create opportunities and conditions for students to actively engage in the participation and self-regulation of learning processes and decision-making, the very nature of student agency is that students choose their roles within their learning process. We cannot force students to take charge of their learning but can only develop the competencies that can support them in directing their learning and making decisions about their learning (e.g., self-regulation, communication) and create the conditions and opportunities for them to experiment with their own agency (setting and tracking goals, etc.).

To create the optimal conditions for student involvement, expression and agency, students need to be viewed as having distinct and meaningful perspectives that can support and enhance educational processes.[10] As discussed in Chapter 4, some educators give pause when involving students in educational processes and decision-making, particularly those relating to assessment, because they question students' capacity or their ability to make the right decisions. As a result, if we want to view students' perspectives as important and meaningful for the teaching and learning process, we also must respectfully and meaningfully *acknowledge the traditional power imbalances that exists within schools*[11] and how this might play a role in how we create the conditions and opportunities for students to be involved, make decisions and have autonomy within classroom assessment processes.

When thinking about creating conditions for student voice, we must consider the role of student leadership. Many scholars argue that student voice consists of a progression from being informed about decisions to making the decisions that lead to reforms in education.[12] With this, many view student leadership as the pinnacle or the goal for students to achieve as this then makes students the decision-makers. However, we find the use of the term 'leadership' problematic as not all students are attracted to the visibility or responsibility of a leadership position but still want to play a meaningful role in being part of the decision-making process. The assumption is that if students want to make decisions and guide change in their schools, then they need to be leaders. However, we know that this is not always the case in everyday life. We have those who are incredible leaders and are, at face value, the decision-makers but in most cases, they have other experts around them who are informing their decision-making so they can present these good decisions. To provide meaningful opportunities for student voice, we must acknowledge that all students have knowledge and experiences that give them valuable insights to inform decisions about learning and teaching processes. While we want to promote student leaders, we also have to be cognisant that not all students will or want to be 'leaders' but they still have the relevant expertise and experience that comes with having meaningful experiences as a student and can contribute in a range of ways.

Despite student voice initiatives which have attempted to create opportunities for students to be part of making important educational decisions, many of the ways in which we engage students and provide opportunities for them to express their ideas or make decisions heavily controlled and guided by adults.[13] This is why involving students in assessment decisions and processes is something that might cause some concern for teachers. While boundaries are needed when we consider ways in which to involve students in assessment processes, we also must be willing to let go of our desire to be in control of the process. We have likely all observed student leadership decisions which have resulted in helping to raise funds to repair the basketball nets, introduce special snacks in the canteen or create a playlist to play before the morning bell. However, we have less likely heard about students making decisions about what and how they are being assessed. For many teachers, they advocate for student voice but only in making decisions that do not cross into the realm of their roles and responsibilities. While we will need to provide clear boundaries on what students can make decisions on, there are ways in which we can provide student voice opportunities, while also creating opportunities for student agency. Next, we present a case study to explore this further.

A case study: Assessment agency

In this section, we draw upon our empirical research to highlight the ways in which assessment agency can be developed and what this might look like in practice. As mentioned in the preface, our first project[14] was about ensuring that students were included in the discussion about:

1 What competencies they felt were most relevant to their future (study and work). Students conducted research on different competencies and attempted to describe what these competencies were.
2 What could be 'observed.' Students reflected on their own performance and the performances of others to determine what could be observed and then articulated in clear language.

The purpose of having students lead the initial design and structure of the frameworks was to give them a sense of agency and acknowledge that their own experiences contribute meaningful and relevant insights into what competencies should be assessed. In our longitudinal project (2023–present), we found that students, who were not part of the initial design process, wanted to have a say about what they thought about competency-based assessment and how they felt it should be implemented. For example, several of the Year 7 and Year 10 students who participated in the focus groups in 2023 felt that learning about competencies and applying them was valuable:

> Well, all those things [competencies] are probably things that you need for the whole of your life and that are probably valuable in all future pathways and things, so I think they are valuable to learn about.
>
> (Year 7 student, focus group, 2023)

Interestingly, the students also provided advice about how they thought they should be involved in the assessment of competencies:

> I think one idea is you choose one of the frameworks that you think is valuable for that subject and then you assess yourself on how you think you displayed that so it's not like "oh I don't think creativity is important in maths" but if creativity is the concept that's applied to maths, then what am I meant to do? So, it's like you can work in a way that works well for you whilst also overall across the board having a variety of experiences.
>
> (Year 7 student, focus group, 2023)

> I think maybe showing us the rubrics like we brought up before so that we can try to demonstrate it, but the teacher can also pick out those things that we did and then assess us in that way would be helpful because we'd then know that we should be doing something.
>
> (Year 7 student, focus group, 2023)

The students wanted to be assessed by their teachers and also have opportunities to self-assess, which demonstrates that learners have clear views about who should assess their work and the value of this. The next phase of our research explores students and their role in competency-based assessment, with a focus on how they track their learning and what they do with descriptors provided in the frameworks to progress their learning. We also want to explore the role of choice (e.g., choosing competencies that they feel align best with a subject) and how teacher and self-assessment can be used in combination to maximise student learning.

Designing and selecting assessment instruments: The co-construction process

One way to reposition students away from being the objects of assessment and towards actively involving them in the assessment process is to include them in the assessment planning and/or design of assessment instruments. The following provide some tangible ways to involve students in the design process.

Brainstorming sessions and student feedback surveys. While seemingly a simple technique, just ask students. Continually and frequently asking for student input as part of an ongoing process will enable us to better understand students' learning experiences and needs. In other words, there is no pre-scribed time to gather information from students (e.g., before or after a unit or term) but it should be part of the learning and teaching process. By gathering information from students about *what* should be assessed (with a focus on what is relevant content), *how* it should be assessed (format, criteria, feedback approaches, etc.) and *when* (frequency, timing, etc.), teachers can gain valuable insights into students' needs and perspectives. The problem is that we often make a lot of assumptions about what students need and want, without really knowing what they need and want. By providing an open forum to discuss the design and selection of assessment instruments, we are able to communicate to students that we value their experiences and insights. While teachers must still identify boundaries around the *what*, *how* and *when* of assessment, given that we are bound to institutional, district, state and/or federal assessment and reporting requirements, there are often opportunities to experiment with the design and selection of assessment instruments within low-stakes, formative assessment tasks.

In our recent longitudinal pilot study, we gathered student perspectives on what they wanted to be assessed on (see Box 6.1).

Box 6.1   Our research reflections: What did students want to be assessed on?

In our recent longitudinal pilot study, we found that students wanted to be assessed on key curriculum content, as they knew that this would prepare them for high-stakes exams, while also developing and tracking competencies. Secondary students who participated in a focus group discussion expressed that they wanted to learn more about competencies, such as problem-solving, critical thinking and communication, *in addition to* the content they needed for their subjects. They argued that if competencies were assessed, and they had clear understanding of how to progress in the targeted competency, then they could develop these *alongside* the content they were learning in their subjects. While we, as the researchers in the study, were not expecting the participating students to express that they wanted to spend more time learning about key competencies and tracking their development over time, particularly given that we could see the value of teaching and assessing competencies but made some assumptions that this might not be something that students might not value at the start of the project. However, the participating students expressed that not only did they recognise the value of teaching and assessing key competencies but they felt that competencies could be assessed alongside the key content they were learning. In other words, felt teaching and assessing competencies would complement their content learning rather than distract from it. We found, firsthand in this project, that when we provide opportunities for students to share their experiences and perspectives, it can be extremely insightful.

By gathering students' perspectives through discussions and surveys, this does not mean that educators are bound to take on every suggestion. It is a starting point rather than a 'to do' list. Teachers must incorporate their own expertise and experiences to create meaningful boundaries that still allow for opportunities to incorporate student perspectives. As a result, student feedback or perception surveys are increasingly being used in schools to gather data on students' beliefs and attitudes towards the quality of their learning experiences. One study, which gathered data on a student perception survey that was administered to students in two Australian secondary schools, found that most teachers did not know how to incorporate or act upon student feedback once they received it.[15] Consequently, the participating students reported that the surveys were of no value because no action was ever taken. Therefore, while teachers must create boundaries around what they can and cannot incorporate in the design and selection of assessment instruments, they must be ready to respond, in some tangible and visible way, to students' comments and suggestions. This is why a lot of thought and care must be taken when gathering students' feedback and suggestions, with clear boundaries already created. Therefore, do not ask students to provide input into aspects that you cannot or are unwilling to change or respond to. There should be a clear purpose as to the rationale for gathering student feedback, which should then be communicated to the students.

Finally, while inviting students to share their experiences and perspectives is important, it is also an opportunity to gather information about how students best learn and what their needs are. In other words, teachers must gather information about the conditions that support and/or deter their ability to maximise their learning (e.g., noise, visual reinforcements). Brainstorming sessions and surveys are a great way to ask about and identify potential barriers that may prevent students from doing their best on their assessment tasks. Chapter 4 suggests ways in which teachers might identify barriers to access (e.g., lengthy and unclear instructions, time limits) and these can be considered when collecting information from students. For example, it is important to determine how students prefer to express their understanding (e.g., written, spoken or multimodal). This is not to say that students should never have to demonstrate their understanding in a mode that they do not prefer. On the contrary, students should be given frequent opportunities to demonstrate their understanding in different ways and be encouraged to develop in areas they feel less confident in. However, providing some element of choice, for *some* assessment tasks, acknowledges that we, as teachers, often favour and over-rely on a particular mode of expression and in doing so deny opportunities to demonstrate understanding in different ways. Providing choice in some assessment tasks, not all, attempts to address this. Additionally, it is important to gather information about how students prefer to track their learning and interact with resources as they may provide insights that educators may not have considered. For example, some students may have insights into how they want to track their progress, such as using checklists, rubrics and/or collaboration with peers. Students' perspectives on how technological tools can be utilised to support them in being able to demonstrate what they know and why may introduce you to tools that you may not have considered but could be helpful in supporting teaching, learning and assessment processes (e.g., speech to text tools, generative AI, online dictionaries). Again, students' suggestions must be filtered in light of your own expertise and experiences and the external factors at play (e.g., time, institutional assessment and reporting requirements and access to resources) but may provide opportunities for meaningful ways to assess learners.

Co-constructed rubrics. When students are involved in the design of assessment rubrics, they are able to understand and/or make decisions about what is assessed (e.g., What are the skills and qualities that are deemed most important to assess for a particular task?) and how (e.g., How must students express their understanding?). When a rubric already exists, or the teacher has prepared a first draft, students can be given an opportunity to examine and provide feedback on how it can be improved for clarity and utility. When examining the rubric, students may be able to identify potential barriers that exist that may make it difficult for them to address the criteria, such as unclear language, confusion in how to progress from one point to another, or accessibility concerns (e.g., requiring students to have typing skills, etc.). It is only through unpacking and going through the rubric together, that teachers and students can come to a shared understanding of what performance should look like and how it should be assessed. This allows for the checking of consistency between the teacher and students in how performance is described and then interpreted. This process provides valuable feedback for both teachers and students. While students can still be part of the co-construction process by having a say and making decisions about existing rubrics, teachers can also develop rubrics from scratch with students.[16] This requires working with students to identify what the focus of the task is and the skills, knowledge and understandings that should be assessed. Through this process, students begin to understand that creating the 'right' language that clearly and concisely reflects performance is difficult as it must be accessible to all students. Co-designing rubrics allows teachers to create the conditions for students to take charge of their learning as they have a much deeper understanding and ownership of what is being assessed. As a result, there is more agreement between teachers and students about marks/results as they have a shared understanding of what they are being assessed on.

While we do not need to reconstruct every rubric for each class and/ or assessment task every year, we can make decisions that are based on the dynamics and needs of our classrooms. The following questions might help in determining whether or not to co-construct your rubric with your students.

1 *Engagement.* Are you looking for an opportunity to engage or re-engage your students in the assessment process? This collective process might open valuable dialogue among the students which could result in increased engagement and ownership of the assessment process.
2 *Accountability.* Do you want to find ways to make your students more accountable and aware of what they are being assessed on? Co-constructing rubrics provides opportunities for shared responsibility for what is being assessed and understanding the reasons why.
3 *Clarity.* Are you wanting to check the clarity and/or readability of the rubric? The co-construction process can help to ensure that criteria are clearly understood by students (e.g., student-friendly wording).
4 *Relevance.* Do you want to ensure that what is being assessed is relevant and meaningful for your students? This is one way to ensure that students understand the value and relevance of what is being assessed and how development in these areas will be advantageous.

Assessment processes: How do we meaningfully involve students in the process?

While involving students in the planning, selection and design of assessment instruments is one way to position students as active participants and decision-makers, there are also ways to encourage involvement, expression and autonomy within the process of completing the assessment task.

Self-regulation. If we actively involve students in the assessment process, we create opportunities for students to take more ownership of their learning in the process of completing the assessment task. While students become part of the decision-making about the design of an assessment instrument, such as the co-design or co-construction of rubrics, it becomes an important tool for self-regulation through the assessment process. If students have a strong grasp of how performance is described and the distinction between the different levels, they can then act and create a plan to develop in their learning and track their progress. They can set goals for themselves, with the support of explicit teaching and support from their teachers. Next, they can identify what they need to know and what tools (e.g., software to support the use of vocabulary) and support (e.g., peers, teachers) they need to achieve this. Finally, they can plan their approach of how to track progress. However, this entire process should be scaffolded by teachers. In our longitudinal pilot project, we

1.1 When communicating, I use feedback by

○ listening to what people say about what I do and use their ideas to make things even better

○ having conversations with others about what I'm saying, and I can use their ideas to make my communication clearer

○ changing how I talk or share things based on what people say, so it's more interesting and makes more sense to everyone

○ ask for advice to make improvements

○ i'm working towards this

○ I don't know

1.2 When communicating, I check my audience understands

○ by asking them questions

○ by looking around and making eye contact and checking their body language to see if they appear to understand.

○ say things in a different way to help everyone get what I mean

○ I'm working towards this

○ I don't know

Figure 6.2 Excerpt from our online self-assessment tool.

created a self-assessment tool that aimed to provide regular opportunities for students to self-assess and track their progress. The self-assessment tool (see Figure 6.2) took the form of an online survey that asked students to identify which criterion description best described their current understanding and/or performance for each of the key indicators. They then were asked to provide evidence of this, providing examples from their work. The tool also encouraged students to reflect on how they might strategise to best work their way up the continuum by identifying what knowledge, skills and strategies they might need to develop and how.

It is important to note that any assessment criteria, whether in a rubric or checklist, should be supported by concrete examples. While discussing the language that describes the performance is the first step, having concrete examples of what the performance looks like can support students' understanding and provide opportunities for self-regulation. By having examples, students can learn to identify how the example relates to the assessment criteria and then compare this to their own work. This process requires students to identify the

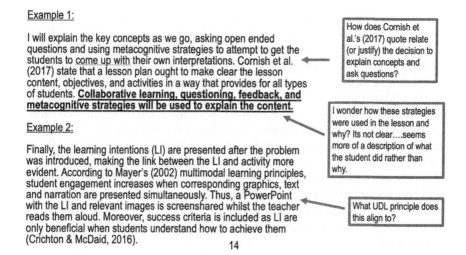

Example 1:

I will explain the key concepts as we go, asking open ended questions and using metacognitive strategies to attempt to get the students to come up with their own interpretations. Cornish et al. (2017) state that a lesson plan ought to make clear the lesson content, objectives, and activities in a way that provides for all types of students. **Collaborative learning, questioning, feedback, and metacognitive strategies will be used to explain the content.**

> How does Cornish et al.'s (2017) quote relate (or justify) the decision to explain concepts and ask questions?

Example 2:

Finally, the learning intentions (LI) are presented after the problem was introduced, making the link between the LI and activity more evident. According to Mayer's (2002) multimodal learning principles, student engagement increases when corresponding graphics, text and narration are presented simultaneously. Thus, a PowerPoint with the LI and relevant images is screenshared whilst the teacher reads them aloud. Moreover, success criteria is included as LI are only beneficial when students understand how to achieve them (Crichton & McDaid, 2016).

> I wonder how these strategies were used in the lesson and why? Its not clear....seems more of a description of what the student did rather than why.

> What UDL principle does this align to?

14

Figure 6.3 Worked example.[17]

alignment to the criteria but also the strengths and next steps needed in their own work. Some teachers have concerns about students becoming too reliant on examples; however, these examples do not have to be full versions of assessment tasks but can be broken down examples that are modified and taught, as worked examples, to students to help them unpack and notice aspects of the example in light of the assessment criteria. Students need to be explicitly taught what is expected before they can take steps to regulate their own learning so they can fully demonstrate their understanding and abilities on the assessment task. Therefore, teachers must create the conditions for students to self-regulate and this begins with explicitly teaching and breaking down what is being assessed and what 'good' performance looks like on the assessment task. This, then, allows students to maximise and regulate their learning through the process of completing the assessment task.

Figure 6.3 provides an example from one of our initial teacher education subjects. In this first-year Bachelor of Education subject, students were required to explain and justify the pedagogical decisions they made in their lesson plan. We provided some examples and then provided annotations to help them consider how the response met the specific criteria in the rubric.

The many approaches to feedback. We all know that providing targeted feedback and guidance to students during the assessment process has a significant impact on learning (see also Chapter 3). However, feedback is most effective when it explicitly states what to do next or how to improve learning, which we often refer to as **feedforward**.[18] Many educators focus on giving task-related feedback that focuses on how well the student addressed the task.[19] While this type of feedback plays an important role, it does not always support students in identifying the strategies and approaches that may help them improve or progress.

The other important factor to consider is what roles students, teachers and peers play in feedback. We have already argued that students need to take charge of their learning by understanding what they are being assessed on and then making plans to progress and track their learning. This aligns with the current pushback against the idea that teachers must drive the feedback process. Scholars argue that students must be actively involved in seeking opportunities for feedback, taking the time to work with feedback and act upon it and then applying this information to future tasks.[20] In addition, students can seek, work with, act upon and apply feedback *together*, through the process of peer feedback. Another way to allow students to express their understanding of their learning within the assessment process is to allow students to drive both teacher–student consultations and teacher–parent–student consultations. Traditionally, teachers present information about where a student is at and where they need to be; however, students are very capable of presenting and expressing this information to others. However, teachers must create the opportunities for students to take charge and make decisions about how they will present their progress to others and decide what evidence of this learning they will use. To support students to do so, teachers must ensure they model and scaffold this process so that students are equipped to confidently present their learning progress to others.

Finally, given that we want students to seek opportunities for feedback, it would be remiss not to mention the opportunities that generative AI might provide. At the time of writing this book, the topic of generative AI has been at the forefront of assessment conversations. While many of these conversations have been about how we ensure that students do not use generative AI to cheat, there have been fewer discussions about how generative AI might be used for feedback purposes. Due to this, ChatGPT was used to ask this very question:

"What are some prompts that I could type into ChatGPT to help me get feedback on my writing?"

This is the response I received:

"Certainly! If you'd like to get feedback on your writing, you can use specific prompts to guide ChatGPT. Here are some prompts you can use:

1 **Overall feedback:**

- "Can you provide general feedback on my writing? What are the strengths and weaknesses you observe?"

2 **Clarity and understanding:**

- "Do you find the main message or thesis of my writing clear? Can you summarise the main points or arguments?"

3 **Organisation and structure:**

- "How is the overall organisation and structure of my writing? Are the paragraphs well-organised and logically connected?"

4 **Specific feedback:**

- "Please point out specific areas where my writing could be improved. Any particular sentences or paragraphs that need attention?"

5 **Consistency and flow:**

- "Does my writing flow smoothly from one point to the next? Are the transitions effective between paragraphs?"

6 **Voice and tone:**

- "Does my writing reflect a consistent voice and tone? Does the tone align with the purpose and intended audience?"

7 **Language and style:**

- "Are there areas where the language could be more concise or precise? Any suggestions for varying sentence structure or enhancing overall style?"

8 **Engagement and impact:**

- "How engaging is my writing? Are there elements that could be added to captivate the reader more?"

9 **Grammar and mechanics:**

- "Did you notice any grammatical errors, typos or punctuation issues? Is the writing free from distracting language issues?"

10 **Formatting and presentation:**

- "How does the overall presentation look? Are headings, subheadings and formatting elements used effectively?"

11 **Suggestions for improvement:**

- "Based on your assessment, what specific suggestions do you have for improving my writing?"

Feel free to customise these prompts based on your specific writing goals and areas of concern. Additionally, you can provide more context or ask for feedback on particular aspects that are most important to you."[21]

While there are concerns that we will need to continue to interrogate and address, such as bias in large language models,[22] in generative AI tools like ChatGPT, technology has the potential to be a valuable feedback tool that engages students to think about the writing process (and other key learning processes as well), as opposed to just fixing their work for them. However, to achieve this, teachers will need to model and lead students in how to use this technology to enhance feedback processes.

Chapter summary and reflection

This chapter explored how actively involving and engaging students can enrich the assessment process and enhance learning. By challenging common misconceptions, we argue that students can meaningfully engage in assessment processes and by doing so develop a deeper understanding of their learning. Students must be given opportunities to actively engage by (1) *participating* in assessment processes and activities, (2) *having a say* about assessment decisions and (3) *taking charge of their learning as part of the assessment process*. In addition to having opportunities to meaningful and actively engage in the assessment process, students also need opportunities to be involved in the design and selection of assessment instruments. As argued in this chapter, there are multiple opportunities to allow learners to be part of the assessment process but teachers play an important role in *creating the conditions* and *providing appropriate access* to the knowledge, skills and tools needed for students to actively participate.

In considering how you might involve learners in the assessment process, reflect on the following:

1 How does your school currently position learners within the assessment process? What are current institutional policies regarding assessment?
2 What opportunities do learners have to shape assessment practices that directly or indirectly involve them?
3 Identify ways in your school and your classroom which learners can have a say in:

   a What they assessed on,
   b When they are assessed,
   c How they are assessed,
   d Who assesses them?

4 Based on your answers above, how might you give students more opportunities to:

   a *participate* in educational processes and activities,
   b *have a say* about education matters and
   c *take charge of their learning?*

Notes

1 Forbes Breaking News. (2023, February 28). *Kaite Porter to witnesses: 'What grade would you give yourself on your performance today?'* [Video file]. YouTube. https://www.youtube.com/watch?v=y7V6X2j0DPk
2 Tejeiro, R.A., Gomez-Vallecillo, J.L., Romero, A.F., Pelegrina, M., Wallace, A., & Emberley, E. (2012). Summative self-assessment in higher education: Implications of its counting towards the final mark. *Electronic Journal of Research in Educational Psychology, 10*(2), 789–812.
3 Andrade, H.L. (2019, August). A critical review of research on student self-assessment. *Frontiers in Education, 4,* 1–13.
4 Sofyan, M., Barnes, M., & Finefter-Rosenbluh, I. (2022). Fair assessment as an aspect of effective teaching: Teachers' and students' perceptions of and positioning

within assessment practices in Indonesian vocational higher education. *Journal of Vocational Education & Training*, 1–23.

5 Kaderavek, J.N., Gillam, R.B., Ukrainetz, T.A., Justice, L.M., & Eisenberg, S.N. (2004). School-age children's self-assessment of oral narrative production. *Communication Disorders Quarterly*, *26*(1), 37–48.

6 Brown, G., & Harris, L.R. (2014). *The future of self-assessment in classroom practice: Reframing self-assessment as a core competency*, *2*(1), 22–30.

7 Lew, M.D., Alwis, W.A.M., & Schmidt, H.G. (2010). Accuracy of students' self-assessment and their beliefs about its utility. *Assessment & Evaluation in Higher Education*, *35*(2), 135–156.

8 Barnes, M. (2022). Framing teacher quality in the Australian media: The circulation of key political messages? *Educational Review*, *74*(7), 1305–1321.

9 Barnes, M. (2021). Policy actors or objects of policy? Teacher candidates' interpretations of 'teacher quality' policy initiatives in Australia. *Teaching and Teacher Education*, *106*, 103440.

10 Cook-Sather, A. (2014). The trajectory of student voice in educational research. *New Zealand Journal of Educational Studies*, *49*(2), 131–148. https://search .informit.org/doi/10.3316informit.842480978608459.

11 Cook-Sather, A., & Hayward, L. (2021). A matter of perspective: The benefits to students, faculty, and future employers of positioning students as consultants on learning and teaching. *College Teaching*, *69*(1), 12–19. https://doi.org/10.1080/ 87567555.2020.1793715.

12 Mitra, D. (2018). Student voice in secondary schools: The possibility for deeper change. *Journal of Educational Administration*, *56*(5), 473–487. https://doi.org/ 10.1108/JEA-01-2018-0007.

13 Lac, V.T., & Cumings Mansfield, K. (2018). What do students have to do with educational leadership? Making a case for centering student voice. *Journal of Research on Leadership Education*, *13*(1), 38–58. https://doi.org/10.1177/ 1942775117743748.

14 Barnes, M., Lafferty, K., & Li, B. (2024). Assessing twenty-first century competencies: Can students lead and facilitate the co-construction process? *Educational Review*, *76*(4), 691–709.

15 Finefter-Rosenbluh, I., Ryan, T., & Barnes, M. (2021). The impact of student perception surveys on teachers' practice: Teacher resistance and struggle in student voice-based assessment initiatives of effective teaching. *Teaching and Teacher Education*, *106*, 103436.

16 Barnes, M., Lafferty, K., & Li, B. (2024). Assessing twenty-first century competencies: Can students lead and facilitate the co-construction process? *Educational Review*, *76*(4), 691–709

17 Barnes, M. (2023, 2 April). Week 6 tutorial slides [Course presentation]. School of Education, La Trobe University. https://lms.latrobe.edu.au/course/view.php?id =128529.

18 Wollenschläger, M., Hattie, J., Machts, N., Möller, J., & Harms, U. (2016). What makes rubrics effective in teacher-feedback? Transparency of learning goals is not enough. *Contemporary Educational Psychology*, *44–45*, 1–11.

19 Hattie, J., & Timperley, H. (2007). The power of feedback. *Review of Educational Research*, *77*(1), 81–112.

20 Nieminen, J.H., Tai, J., Boud, D., & Henderson, M. (2022). Student agency in feedback: Beyond the individual. *Assessment & Evaluation in Higher Education*, *47*(1), 95–108. https://doi.org/10.1080/02602938.2021.1887080.

21 OpenAI. (2024). ChatGPT (January 26 version) [Large language model]. https:// chat.openai.com/chat.

22 UNESCO, IRCAI. (2024). *Challenging systematic prejudices: An investigation into gender bias in large language models*. UNESCO. https://unesdoc.unesco.org/ ark:/48223/pf0000388971.

Glossary

Agency The capacity of students to make choices, set goals and take responsibility for their education, which in turn, fosters a sense of ownership and empowerment in the learning process.

Agentic engagement Students' proactive initiatives and actions to have a say in how things are taught and what they learn.

Alignment The strategic planning of instructional objectives, teaching strategies and assessment methods to ensure they collectively support the attainment of desired learning outcomes.

Assessment as learning An assessment process where students actively engage in assessing their own knowledge, skills and understanding as part of their learning journey, typically for the purpose of self-monitoring and taking responsibility for their own learning progress.

Assessment for learning An assessment process used to monitor and provide feedback on students' knowledge, skills and understanding during the instructional period, typically for the purpose of supporting and enhancing ongoing learning and development.

Assessment of learning An assessment process used to evaluate and document students' knowledge, skills and understanding at the end of an instructional period, typically for the purpose of grading or determining competence in a particular domain/subject.

Behavioural engagement Students' observable actions, involvement and participation in class activities.

Ceiling effect The ceiling effect occurs when a measure is unable to distinguish differences among subjects at the upper end of the scale, resulting in a clustering of scores at the maximum level and limiting the ability to accurately assess higher levels of performance or ability.

Criterion-referenced Criterion-referenced assessment compares an individual's performance to a predetermined standard or set of criteria, focusing on mastery of specific skills or knowledge rather than comparing performance to that of others.

Cognitive engagement Students' mental effort, focus and active participation in learning tasks.

Common assessment tasks   An assessment task that involves collaboration among a group of teachers to measure the performance of students across different classrooms and/or schools.

Competency   The knowledge, skills, attitudes, values and behaviours stu dents need to thrive in and shape their world, whether that be in future studies, employment or active participation as a global citizen.

Competency-based assessment   Competency-based assessment is an approach that focuses on assessing individuals' proficiency and mastery of specific skills, knowledge and abilities, emphasising the demonstration of competence.

Construct   A construct refers to an abstract concept or characteristic that is targeted for measurement, such as a skill, knowledge area, or attribute, often defined by a set of observable behaviours or indicators.

Data   Systematically collected information, including quantitative and qualitative observations, student performance metrics and feedback, used to inform instructional decision-making, monitor progress and evaluate outcomes.

Diagnostic assessment   An assessment process used to evaluate students' existing knowledge, skills and understanding before or during the instructional period, typically for the purpose of identifying learning needs, strengths and areas for improvement to inform teaching strategies and support personalised learning.

Dichotomous data   A type of categorical data with only two possible values for each observation, also known as binary or yes/no data.

Disposable assessment task   A disposable assessment task is a one-time evaluation instrument designed to measure specific learning outcomes or competencies within a limited context and typically is shared between the student–teacher dyad only.

Emotional (affective) engagement   Students' feelings, attitudes and emotional connection to the learning experience.

Equitable opportunities   When opportunities are equitable, fairness and justice are promoted by actively attempting to eliminate discrimination and provide each student with what they need to succeed.

Evidence   Documented information, observations, artifacts or performances that demonstrate students' understanding, skills, progress or achievement in relation to specific learning objectives or standards.

Extraneous   In the context of cognitive load theory, extraneous refers to elements that are not essential to the learning process and can potentially hinder the acquisition and retention of new information.

Far transfer   Refers to the application and utilisation of learned knowledge, skills or strategies in contexts that are significantly different from those in which they were initially acquired, demonstrating deep understanding and adaptability.

Feedforward   Providing student guidance and next steps to improve understanding.

Floor effect The floor effect occurs when a measure is unable to distinguish differences among subjects at the lower end of the scale, resulting in a clustering of scores at the minimum level and limiting the ability to accurately assess lower levels of performance or ability.

General capabilities General capabilities in teaching, learning and assessment refer to a broad range of knowledge, skills and dispositions that are essential for students to succeed in learning, work and life, encompassing areas such as critical and creative thinking, ethical understanding, intercultural competence and personal and social capability.

Grain size Refers to the level of detail or specificity at which learning objectives, instructional activities or assessment tasks are defined, ranging from broader, overarching concepts to more narrowly focused, discrete skills or knowledge components.

Guttman chart A visual representation that displays the hierarchical ordering of items or skills based on the pattern of responses, indicating the extent to which individuals possess the underlying abilities or traits being measured.

High-road transfer Refers to the application and transfer of learned knowledge, skills or strategies to novel and complex situations, requiring deep understanding, critical thinking and problem-solving abilities.

Honour systems A system that allows individuals, like students, freedom without constant supervision. It relies on the trust that those who are granted this freedom will follow rules and not misuse the trust placed in them.

Inclusive education An educational approach that aims to create learning environments where all students, regardless of their differences, backgrounds or abilities, feel that they are valued, respected and included in the learning process.

Low-road transfer Refers to the automatic and effortless application of learned knowledge, skills or strategies to familiar and routine tasks or situations, often occurring without conscious awareness or deliberate effort.

Moderation A collaborative process among educators to review and adjust assessment standards, practices and judgements to ensure fairness, consistency and validity across different contexts, teachers and students.

Near transfer Refers to the application and transfer of learned knowledge, skills or strategies to contexts that share similarities or common elements with the original learning context, typically requiring some adaptation or modification.

Nested assessment Involves the integration of multiple levels or layers of assessment tasks and criteria within a broader framework, allowing for the evaluation of both specific skills or knowledge components and overall learning outcomes.

Non-disposable assessment task A non-disposable assessment task is an evaluative instrument designed to measure specific learning outcomes or competencies that can be reused for subsequent assessments or learning experiences, providing ongoing opportunities for students to demonstrate their understanding and skills development.

Norm-referenced Compares an individual's performance to the performance of a larger group (norm group), typically yielding scores that indicate how an individual's performance ranks relative to others rather than measuring mastery of specific learning objectives.

Partial credit data Refers to information that acknowledges and assigns value to partially correct or incomplete responses provided by students, allowing for a more nuanced evaluation of their understanding and skills beyond simple correctness or incorrectness.

Plasticity The brain's ability to reorganise and adapt by forming new neural connections over time.

Positivist paradigm A perspective that emphasises the use of empirical evidence and scientific methods to study and understand educational phenomena, focusing on observable facts and measurable outcomes to inform teaching practices and assessments.

Practicality The ease and feasibility with which an assessment can be designed, administered, scored and interpreted, taking into account available resources, money, time and context.

Psychometric testing Based within the field of psychology, this type of assessment is focused on the measurement of psychological attributes, abilities and traits.

Reliability Reliability in assessment refers to the consistency and stability of assessment results over time, across different observers, or alternative forms of the assessment.

Running record A running record is an assessment used to assess student reading as they read aloud with a focus on word accuracy, errors and their use of reading strategies.

Standards-referenced Compares an individual's performance to a predetermined set of criteria or standards, measuring the extent to which they have achieved specific learning objectives or competencies regardless of the performance of others.

Student participation Students actively taking part in educational activities, events and decision-making processes.

Student voice The meaningful expression of students' perspectives, opinions and ideas in matters related to their education and school environment.

Understanding by Design An educational framework that emphasises designing a curriculum backwards from the desired learning outcomes, focusing on identifying enduring understandings, essential questions and assessment methods to promote deep understanding and transfer of knowledge.

Validity Validity in assessment refers to the degree to which an assessment accurately measures what it is intended to measure.

Worked example A step-by-step demonstration of how to solve a problem or perform a task.

Index

Note: **Bold** page numbers refer to tables and *italic* page numbers refer to figures.

For Product Safety Concerns and Information please contact our EU representative GPSR@taylorandfrancis.com Taylor & Francis Verlag GmbH, Kaufingerstraße 24, 80331 München, Germany

Printed and bound by CPI Group (UK) Ltd, Croydon, CR0 4YY
08/06/2025
01897000-0015